New Mexico's Troubled Years

CHARLES BENT

MILITARY GOVERNOR OF NEW MEXICO, 1846-47

New Mexico's Troubled Years

THE STORY OF THE EARLY
TERRITORIAL GOVERNORS

by Calvin Horn

WITH A FOREWORD BY

John F. Kennedy

ALBUQUERQUE: HORN & WALLACE, PUBLISHERS

The material in *New Mexico's Troubled Years* is based upon a series of articles by Calvin Horn published and copyrighted in *New Mexico Magazine,* Department of Development, Santa Fe, under the following dates: June, October, 1957; April, October, 1958; March, April, November, 1959; September 1961, January, September, October, 1963. Portraits of the governors are reproduced through the courtesy of the Museum of New Mexico.

This is the 8th title issued under the publisher's imprint.

Manufactured in the United States of America
Library of Congress Catalog Card No. 63-20439
FIRST EDITION

Horn & Wallace, Publishers
P.O. Box 4204, Albuquerque, New Mexico

TO RUTH, MY WIFE

Contents

Foreword

THE HISTORY OF NEW MEXICO IS A DISTILLATION OF THE American experience. It provides striking evidence of the truth of Walt Whitman's dictum: "Here is not merely a nation but a teeming Nation of nations." For New Mexico offers a compact illustration of the way a diversity of races and cultures pooled their traditions and skills to build an American state—and, in doing so, displayed impressive qualities of courage and resourcefulness.

New Mexico's history goes back many centuries to the time when the Pueblo Indians, confronted by drought, disease and hostile tribes, developed a civilization only a little less advanced than those of the Aztec and the Maya to the south. Then the conquistadores of Spain, laboring valiantly across trackless plains, wove a new strand into the New Mexican fabric. Mexicans and Yankees soon made their distinctive contributions. Today New Mexico stands as an example of the ability of people of diverse backgrounds to live and work together in amity.

This volume tells the story of New Mexico's first years within the United States. These were stirring and picturesque times, but they were also times of uncertainty and peril. The early governors faced hard problems in establishing law, justice and a stable framework of society on a tough and undisciplined frontier. Acting without precedent, under conditions that required immediate decision, they had to improvise, trying to bring calm out of chaos, equity out of vigilantism. With the advantage of hindsight, we can discover many instances where they might have acted more wisely. Nevertheless, they deserve to have their trials and their accomplishments preserved in the record of our nation's history.

In these formative years, New Mexico was dependent on the national government for almost total support. We can be proud that the investment of the people of the United States in New Mexico is today paying dividends to free people everywhere. The largest known deposits of uranium in the world are in New Mexico, along with important reserves of oil, copper and timber. The state is celebrated for its atomic and space research facilities. Yet the scenic grandeur on every hand forever reminds us of New Mexico's foundations in the past. Not the least of New Mexico's resources is the quiet spectacle of yesterday dwelling in harmony with tomorrow— a spectacle which offers the hope of a brighter future for men and women all over the world.

JOHN F. KENNEDY

The White House
July 1963

New Mexico's Troubled Years

Introduction

THE OFFICE OF GOVERNOR IS AN ANCIENT ONE IN NEW Mexico. For more than three and a half centuries it has been in continuous existence—under the Spanish, Mexican, United States and Confederate flags. New Mexico had its first governor, Juan de Oñate, twenty-two years before the arrival of the Pilgrims at Plymouth Rock.

During the first two and a half centuries, New Mexico governors were appointed by a monarch in Madrid, by a dictator in Mexico City, or by a military commander in Washington. Authority for all governors from 1598 until 1851 came from countries far away—in time, in distance.

Inhabitants of New Mexico acknowledged government imposed upon them from without. This was the accepted way in New Mexico. The citizens did not know otherwise. The revolutionary trends that exploded in New England had no counterpart in New Mexico. New Mexicans humbly submitted to foreign dictation. Because of their habit of submission, they had no opportunity to participate in government or to learn of representative government. Early government leaders in New Mexico had no interest in public education, for that might upset the existing domination.

The citizens' only adventure in participation was an occasional bloody revolution. For example, during the American military period, Gen. Stephen Watts Kearny had appointed Charles Bent the first American governor of New Mexico. On January 19, 1847, Bent was murdered—pierced by arrows and scalped—in his Taos home. There were other unpleasant incidents; in several of them the citizens expressed their dissatisfaction in the only way open to them—violence.

The citizens of New Mexico were totally unprepared for American democracy when James S. Calhoun became the first territorial governor of New Mexico on March 3, 1851. He opened his inaugural address:

> An era in the history of New Mexico commenced this day. The problem as to the capacity of the people for self government is to be solved. . . .

The new era in New Mexico brought with it troubled years. When any new country, state or territory comes into being, there are troubled years, but in New Mexico the dramatic change brought conflict, murder and bloodshed. *New Mexico's Troubled Years* is the story of the struggle to bring representative government to a people completely unfamiliar with the concept of democracy.

The story of these years—1851 to 1881—is recorded in the administrations of ten territorial governors. The problems of the first territorial governors in that wild frontier region seem incredible today. Securing the basic necessities for minimal, decent daily existence was a constant struggle. The governors had the additional problem of coping with criminal elements who streamed in to take advantage of the inefficient enforcement of law in the territory. Appointed by Presidents, the territorial governors were, for the most part, men of integrity and high principles. They were variously motivated by patriotic zeal, love of adventure, the possibility of a seat in the United States Senate, a desire for wealth, or a combination of these.

The first of the governors bore a famous name—James S. Calhoun. Dignified, sharp-spoken, he served his nation well and gave his life to the job. Broken in health, he died while crossing the plains on the way back to Washington. He lies in an unmarked grave in a pauper's plot in Kansas City.

Another, Dr. William Carr Lane, gave up a large practice in St. Louis because of a personal tragedy, and accepted the office of governor of New Mexico in the hope that serving his country on the raw frontier would offer a new life. His administration spanned the border trouble over the Mesilla Valley Territory—a dispute that was not settled until the Gadsden Purchase was consummated.

Another, David Meriwether—successful farmer, family man and U.S. Senator—returned to New Mexico thirty-four years after he had spent a month in irons in the dungeon in the Palace of the Governors in Santa Fe, charged by the Mexican government with spying for the United States. Appointed as a "trouble shooter" by President Franklin Pierce, Meriwether brought exacting administration to a territory plagued by Indian wars and political problems.

And so it goes. The parade of governors across the broad tapestry of history presents a colorful picture of the years of struggle and growth in New Mexico. These were strong men in times that called for strong men.

The thirty-year period covered in *New Mexico's*

Troubled Years records the taming of New Mexico and its people by the westward expansion of the United States, by pioneering United States officials, and by the coming of the railroad.

The new era mentioned by Governor Calhoun in 1851 closed with the coming of the railroad to New Mexico in 1881. The railroad created new towns along its trail, by-passing and eclipsing the old towns dating back to Spanish colonial times.

Lew Wallace, the last of the pioneering governors, came to New Mexico by bone-breaking buckboard, taking two days to cover the last one hundred and thirty miles by stage-coach. Three years later, in 1881, Governor Wallace departed New Mexico by Pullman car.

With the close of Lew Wallace's administration, the iron invader and the business men it brought had tamed the outlaw and the Indian. The coming of the railroad was a major factor in creating a state of society in which the six-shooter was not tolerated, outlaws were jailed, and life was safe and secure.

And yet, the heroic effort needed to bring democracy to New Mexico was neither the first nor the only struggle in the territory. The long, recorded history of the area is one of struggle.

The Pueblo Indians of New Mexico first struggled to build their civilization against the elements of nature, disease, and incursions of hostile, nomadic tribes. Vacated Indian ruins throughout New Mexico attest to the struggle to survive waged constantly by the Pueblo Indians centuries ago. A second cultural base was established in New Mexico upon the arrival of the Spanish. On February 23, 1540, Francisco Vásquez de Coronado marched north from Mexico, in search of seven legendary cities of gold. In the party were gold-seekers, adventurers, and priests who intended to establish missions and convert the Indians to the Christian faith. Coronado's expedition departed only forty-eight years after Columbus discovered America. The name, *New Mexico,* was first applied to the region in 1565 by Francisco de Ibarra.

In 1598, a wealthy mine owner, Don Juan de Oñate, established four hundred permanent settlers in New Mexico and became their governor. His capital was San Gabriel, across the Rio Grande from San Juan Pueblo in northern New Mexico.

It is interesting that the first published history of any part of the present states of the Union concerned New Mexico. In 1610, Gaspar Pérez de Villagrá published his *Historia de la Nueva Mexico,* still a standard source for the history of Spanish colonial New Mexico.

The Spanish struggled to govern New Mexico in spite of grave problems with hostile Indians and difficulties of communication and supply; somehow, they held on until the coming of United States troops under Stephen Watts Kearny in August 1846, except for the twelve years of the Pueblo Rebellion which began in 1680. In that year, a Tewa medicine man named Popé aroused in the Pueblo Indians a spirit of freedom which led to a revolt against the Spanish. Europeans were killed or forced to flee. New Mexico was not reconquered until Don Diego de Vargas fought his way back to the Palace of the Governors in Santa Fe in 1692. Thus matters stood until the arrival of the United States Army of the West.

The cultural heritages of the Indian and the Spaniard were joined with the Anglo-Saxon institutions of the United

States upon the arrival of General Kearny's forces in 1846.

The introduction of democracy and free government to a people not familiar with such institutions presented many problems. With poverty and illiteracy widespread, it was little wonder that establishing a workable territorial government was a long and frequently vexing task.

Throughout the period, there was the constant and sometimes painful problem of the amalgamation of three diverse cultures. Lines of communication and transportation had to be established in the vast area, and New Mexico's domestic problems were only a part of the pressures encountered by her early territorial governors.

Advancement was slow—so slow that Daniel Webster, Secretary of State, and C. M. Conrad, Secretary of War, suggested that the United States withdraw from the territory, allowing New Mexico to revert to its native inhabitants! This proposal, however tempting it may have been to Departments of State and War constantly receiving bad news and requests for aid from the young territory, was not taken seriously. It was not in the pioneering spirit of those days.

Besides internal difficulties, the territory was harrassed by many factors influencing national politics. In 1850, for instance, it seemed to fit national policy for New Mexico to become a slave state, but New Mexico did not desire slavery. For this reason, statehood was denied. Although New Mexico desired only to be let alone during the Civil War, the territory was the scene of two bloody Civil War battles. It required some sixty years and the introduction in the Congress of more than fifty acts before New Mexico finally became a state in 1912.

It was the leadership and dedication of these governors which eventually brought respect and understanding for representative government to the people of New Mexico. The early years in New Mexico were years of anguish as the territory gradually moved toward maturity. Within a few years New Mexico caught up with the nineteenth century and became a respectable territory. Today, however, thanks to ten pioneering territorial governors and many other leaders, the State of New Mexico is a present-day showcase for a troubled world to see and—perhaps—to imitate.

JAMES S. CALHOUN

ONE

Vanguard of Democracy

JAMES S. CALHOUN

1851-52

O NE COMPANY OF ARTILLERY AND ONE COMPANY OF infantry escorted James S. Calhoun to the Government House in Santa Fe to become the first territorial governor of New Mexico on March 3, 1851. He opened his inaugural address:

> An era in the history of New Mexico commenced this day. The problem as to the capacity of the people for self government is to be solved, preparatory to the assuming of a higher and more glorious position as one of the sovereign and independent states of the Union. . . .

Territorial government of New Mexico, authorized by the Organic Act passed by Congress the preceding September, replaced a confused situation which had existed in New Mexico since Gen. Stephen Watts Kearny conquered New Mexico in the summer of 1846. General Kearny, acting under military orders, took possession of New Mexico and set up a civil government based upon a series of statutes known as the Kearny Code.

Congress debated whether a military general had the authority to establish a civil government. It was argued that

"Gen. Kearny . . . was not only a gallant soldier, but an intelligent gentleman; yet he had unquestionably exceeded his authority and powers" by establishment of temporary governments in some of the provinces.[1]

President James Polk added to the confusion by stating, on July 24, 1848:

> These temporary governments necessarily ceased to exist with the signing of the peace treaty with Mexico . . . until Congress shall act, the inhabitants will be without an organized government. Should they be left in this condition, confusion and anarchy will be likely to prevail.[2]

And yet New Mexico was left in that condition until the appointment of James S. Calhoun as the first territorial governor.

Calhoun was forty-nine years old when he was inaugurated territorial governor of New Mexico, the first of seventeen territorial governors. He had already spent twenty months in New Mexico as Indian agent, serving first under William Medill and then under Luke Lea, Indian commissioners in Washington. At the time of his appointment as governor, he was awaiting a reply to a letter he had written to Lea on December 28, 1850:

> The Utahs seem to be perfectly quiet, and say they are waiting to ascertain what their Great Father, the President of the United States, will do for them. Many of the Pueblo Indians inquire why it is their Great Father will not allow them to visit him.[3]

Calhoun had served with Zachary Taylor in the Mexican War, 1846-48, and it was President Taylor who had appointed him the first Indian agent of New Mexico. After Taylor's death, July 9, 1850, Calhoun continued to serve.

James Calhoun had left a serene and prosperous existence in Georgia to take the post. He had owned a little steamship line, plying between Havana and the mainland. He had been a director of two banks and of the Chattahoochee Railroad. He had served three terms in the legislature and three in the senate of Georgia, and a term as mayor of Columbus.[4]

Now, as Indian agent in New Mexico, he found himself dealing with several groups of difficult, even hostile, Indians. Washington was distant, and the funds, supplies and authority he required often came too little and too late. Much of his time as Indian agent had been occupied with exact reports to Washington, appeals for help, and anxieties for the people in his care.

One matter that had particularly concerned Agent Calhoun was the fate of the White family. In October 1849, Apaches killed J. M. White, a prominent merchant of Santa Fe, and several other men, but took as captives Mrs. White, her young daughter, and a colored servant. Pueblo Indians reported seeing the child in the camp of the Apaches. Mrs. White's brother had information that "the child is certainly alive, that the traders who go among the Indians see it frequently . . . they have offered thousands of dollars, and say that it cannot be ransomed at any price."[5]

Calhoun was determined that the mystery of the fate of Mrs. White and her daughter be cleared up. He had written Indian Commissioner William Medill about the capture:

> I have just secured the services of a Mexican trader, who knows the Apaches well, their haunts and trails . . . I promised to pay him one thousand dollars, and other gratuities, if he succeeds in bringing in Mrs. White and

her daughter . . . if the money promised was the last
cent I could command on earth, and I was without hope
of reimbursements, it would not be the less promptly paid
upon the happening of the contingency which induced the
reward.[6]

The fate of Mrs. White and her daughter[7] and the
Washington invitation for the Utahs were two of the pre-
occupations of James Calhoun. However, when the mail arrived in Santa Fe February 26, 1851, Calhoun was not to
receive the requested invitation for his Utahs, but rather a
letter from Daniel Webster, Secretary of State:

DEPARTMENT OF STATE
WASHINGTON, JANUARY 9, 1851

SIR:

The president having, by and with the advice of the
Senate, appointed you to be the Governor of the Territory
of New Mexico, I have the honor to enclose your commission. You will be pleased to inform the Department of the
receipt of it, and, should it be accepted, of the name of the
State or County in which you were born.

I am, Sir, respectfully,

Your obedient servant,
DANIEL WEBSTER[8]

Calhoun accepted the appointment and was inaugurated. During the ninety days that followed, giant strides
were taken toward the formation of a complete, function-
ing, democratic government in an area where chaos and
ambiguity had existed.

In this brief formative period, Calhoun hoped to stop
Indian depredations which he had been unable to control
in the twenty months preceding. As governor, commander
in chief and Indian superintendent, he now had a great

deal of authority. On March 18, he issued a proclamation to
the people:

> I recommend to all able-bodied male citizens of the
> Territory, capable of bearing arms, the formation of volun-
> teer corps to protect their families, property and homes,
> and, as Commander in Chief . . . will commission the
> officers of such companies. . . .[9]

He wrote to Indian Commissioner Lea, four days later:

> I seize the opportunity to inform you that Indian
> murders and depredations are almost daily occurring in
> this Territory, South and West of Santa Fe.[10]

The following week, he wrote to President Millard
Fillmore:

> Until the Apaches and Navajos are completely sub-
> dued, we can neither have quiet or prosperity in this Ter-
> ritory. You are aware that our Treasury is empty, and that
> we are without munitions of war.[11]

Two days later, he appealed to H. H. Stuart, Secretary
of the Interior:

> We need munitions of war of every kind. These we
> have not, and our Treasury is empty. Has Congress pro-
> vided the means to aid us? If I had the means at this
> moment, I could, in a few months, secure a lasting peace
> with the Indians of this Territory, and locate them within
> fixed limits. . . .[12]

Meanwhile, with the precision of a military commander, Calhoun undertook four steps necessary to form a
democratic government, where none had existed. As a first
step, a census had to be taken. On March 12, Calhoun ordered the first census of the territory. He promised to ask

the territorial legislature for an appropriation to pay the census workers. A month later, the census was complete, with 56,984 citizens counted in the new territory.[13]

The second matter claiming the governor's attention was the apportionment of thirteen senators, or *councilors* as they were called, and twenty-six representatives designated by the Organic Act among the eight existing loosely-organized districts within the territory. Governor Calhoun requested his secretary, David W. Whiting, to work out the apportionment. David Whiting wrote in his diary:

> The districts of Taos, Rio Arriba, Valencia, and Socorro have the largest surplus; the odd senators were accorded to them. The counties of Rio Arriba and Valencia having the largest surplus; the odd representatives were accorded to them.[14]

In the House of Representatives, Taos and Rio Arriba had five representatives each; Santa Fe, four; San Miguel, Valencia and Bernalillo, three each; Socorro, two; Santa Ana, one. Senators, or councilors, were apportioned: Rio Arriba, five; San Miguel and Socorro, three each; Bernalillo, two.[15]

The census and apportionment completed, the third step in organizing territorial government was the election of representatives to the first territorial legislature. Governor Calhoun set the election for May 19, 1851. His secretary wrote, after the election:

> Received complaints from several sources that the election has been illegally carried on . . . soldiers having voted, and that not only once, but often three or four times, teamsters and others not residing in the territory were allowed to vote; and even lads not over 14 years of age

were allowed to take the oath and drop their tickets in the ballot box.[16]

These difficulties, although distressing to the administration of the new territory, were scarcely unique. And, in fact, Governor Calhoun had some vigorous recommendations to make on the subject of election abuses in his opening address to the territorial legislature.

The climax of the ninety-day period was to be June 2, 1851, when Governor Calhoun intended to convene the legislature. However, on that day a majority of legislators failed to appear. The following day, June 3, the legislature organized. Calhoun's address was read to the body.

Calhoun discussed all the issues of his day. Touching upon the complaints of vote frauds, he said:

> There is nothing more corrupting or dangerous to the liberties of the people, than frauds committed under the assumed guise of personal rights. . . . It is our solemn duty, so to guard the rights of our citizens, that is, the people of the Territory, that their own votes shall reflect their own purposes. . . . I suggest the propriety of a law which shall require each voter to register his name prior to an election.

On capital punishment:

> Humanity shudders at the thought of capital punishments, but I am not prepared to recommend [its] entire abolition at this time. The day is near at hand, I trust, when you will be prepared to substitute an effective remedy for such punishments.

On pardons:

> The subject of commuting punishments is an important one, which I commend to your consideration.

On gambling:

> The serious evils of gambling are daily seen, and if it could be accomplished, its entire prohibition would contribute immensely to the peace and happiness of society.

On education (in a territory where seven-eighths of the population was illiterate) :

> The subject of education will not fail to command a full share of your consideration. Unless the people are educated and enlightened, you may, in vain, expect a sound morality to prevail, either in public or private life. A government in which ignorance and vice prevail, can neither be stable or prosperous. . . . I recommend you to memorialize Congress, and respectfully ask for such an appropriation as will be equal to what has been granted to other territories for schools. . . .

> I regard it as important to establish female seminaries, as to educate the Sons of New Mexico. Unless our females are wise and virtuous, there can be no refinement in society, and men will imbrute themselves. Every interest of society demands that a proper system of education should be established without delay.

On welfare:

> Dependence and degradation are inseparable, and poison the very foundation of honesty, truth and virtue. If these assumptions are true, should not wise legislators seek to remedy the evils consequent upon poverty. . . . Let us, at the very commencement of our career in self government, take special care of the weak and the innocent, and secure to them the means of an honest and virtuous independence, the surest shield of probity and morality.[17]

At the close of the governor's address, the legislature set to work and American democracy came to New Mexico.

As a result of urging the legislature to pass a law preventing the entrance of free Negroes into the new territory, Calhoun projected himself into the acrimonious slavery controversy of the day, and became the center of a bitter storm of newspaper and public comment at a later date.

In the summer of 1851, only a few months after his inauguration, Calhoun fell ill and requested permission for a vacation. By the end of August, however, he had given up any hope of leave because of pressing problems in the territory.

In addition to his ill health and Indian trouble, Calhoun faced yet another trial when his political enemies circulated a petition in the territory, concerning the governor's opposition to the election of Capt. A. W. Raynolds, assistant quartermaster of troops stationed in New Mexico, as a delegate to Congress. Of Calhoun, the petition said, in part, "the whole power and influence of his office has been prostituted from what was its proper end and aim."[18]

Calhoun, first in his position as Indian agent, and later as superintendent of Indian affairs for the territory, which office devolved upon him as territorial governor,[19] had been plagued with difficulties with the Army. The trouble hinged upon a conflict of authority and dated back to 1849 when the control of Indians passed from the military to the Department of Interior. When the transfer became known, Col. John Munroe, the commander of troops stationed in New Mexico, immediately cut off all military supplies from Calhoun's order. Continued friction between Munroe and Calhoun resulted in the former being relieved of duty. Munroe's successor as Commander of the Military Department of New Mexico, Col. E. V. Sumner, arrived in Santa Fe on July 19, 1851. On that day, Colonel Sumner refused Governor Calhoun's request that the colonel issue rations to civil prisoners

of the territory. Further, Sumner refused to give escort to
Calhoun for a proposed visit to the Gila Apaches. Sumner
also opposed the giving of presents to Indians, and he de-
plored the necessity for having territorial volunteers serving
under his jurisdiction. It seemed evident that the clear direc-
tives from the Departments of Interior and Army needed to
resolve the conflict were not forthcoming. In consequence,
the difficulties continued.

Governor Calhoun, weakened by an attack of scurvy
and seriously concerned about Indian depredations, wrote
Daniel Webster a letter dated February 29, 1852:

> . . . if such outrages continue much longer, our Ter-
> ritory, instead of becoming settled with an industrious and
> thriving population, will be left in a howling wilderness,
> with no other inhabitants than the wolf, and the birds of
> prey, hovering over the mangled remains of our murdered
> countrymen.[20]

Earlier, Calhoun had described the Payutahs:

> . . . who inhabit the country east of the Sierra Nev-
> ada, are Utahs proper, benumbed by cold, and enfeebled,
> intellectually and physically, by the food upon which they
> subsist, it consisting only of roots, vermin, insects of all
> kinds and everything that creeps, crawls, swims, flies or
> bounds, they may chance to overtake—and when these re-
> sources fail them, and they can find no stranger, they feed
> upon their own children—such a people should not be
> permitted to live within the limits of the United States, and
> must be elevated in the scale of human existence or ex-
> terminated.[21]

Calhoun continued his struggle to secure the cooperation and assistance of the military in handling the Indian

problem which he saw as a continuing threat to the lives and property of the citizens of the territory. The governor was seldom able to agree with Colonel Sumner on strategy. Calhoun wrote to Luke Lea early in April 1852:

> I further assert that the lives of the citizens of the Territory are in imminent danger if Colonel Sumner insists in carrying out his views to withdraw his main force from the Settlements for the purpose of making a campaign in person to the Apache Country. . . . I have deemed it advisable for every American female to leave the country with as little delay as possible.[22]

As Calhoun prepared to evacuate the women and children from Santa Fe, he appealed directly to Colonel Sumner on April 7:

> You are perhaps advised of my weak, feeble, and almost hopeless condition, and I feel that I am speaking almost as a dying man—yet I feel desirous of doing all in my power to promote the public weal.[23]

On this occasion, Sumner agreed with Calhoun's estimate of the situation and decided against the Apache campaign, removing Calhoun's immediate concern and making the planned evacuation unnecessary.

However, the governor's physical condition became critical and was perhaps aggravated by severe attacks upon his character. In the *National Era,* an anti-slavery newspaper with the largest circulation in the nation, had appeared on February 26:

> Governor Calhoun of New Mexico is no better than an infamous kidnapper. Gangs of traders, with licenses bearing his name, authorizing them to purchase Indian

children as slaves for the benefit of persons in New Mexico, have lately been driven out of the Territory of Utah.

These charges appear to have been unsubstantiated.

Apparently believing, as he had stated to Colonel Sumner, that he was a dying man, Calhoun employed native carpenters to build a coffin to his order. By the end of April 1852, the coffin was finished.

To James Calhoun's friends, the governor appeared physically broken and weary of spirit when he was helped into the stage May 6, 1852, in Santa Fe, to begin the long-delayed vacation. He planned to visit Washington and his home in Georgia. In the governor's entourage were his two daughters and their husbands, his secretary, five Pueblo Indians, a military escort of twenty men and the coffin that had been delivered to him.

As he left New Mexico, Calhoun could review several achievements. Chief among these was his work toward creating democratic government in New Mexico. Under his leadership, the first territorial legislature, acting without a constitution, passed an act called The Rights of the People. The act contained twenty sections, enumerating in careful and comprehensive detail the rights of citizens.

James Calhoun had worked for three years to win the friendship of the untamed Apaches, Comanches and Navajos. He had not succeeded, but he had learned to understand them and to know the necessary means of controlling them. He repeatedly urged placing these groups on reservations. The government was to act upon his recommendations, but not until many years had passed.[24]

Calhoun had, however, succeeded in winning the respect and confidence of the native New Mexican people, former Mexican citizens, and civilized Pueblo Indians for himself and, thereby, for the government of the United States.

By traveling constantly in New Mexico, he came to know the territory well and he reported to Washington, fully and often, the exact state of affairs in the territory. He constantly urged the measures and means required to solve the most pressing problem, that of protecting the people and their livestock from Indians.

As Calhoun had anticipated, the vacation trip was to be his last. The hardships of the trail proved too great for a suffering body and an anguished mind, and the great courage that had helped him to face enemies as cruel and tasks as great as any man's, was not enough to see him home. Somewhere on the plains of Kansas, he died. His companions placed his body in the accompanying coffin and carried it to Independence, Missouri.

Only a mortuary at the eastern end of the Santa Fe Trail officially recorded his passing: "The corpse of Governor Calhoun, who died on the road from Santa Fe to Kansas, was bro't in for burial. . . ."[25]

Governor Calhoun had found rest, but the troublesome and troubled Territory of New Mexico continued to clamor for attention.

NOTES

1. U.S. Congress, *The Congressional Globe,* Vol. 19, 30 Congress, First Session, Washington, Blair & Rives, 1848.

2. U.S. Congress, *The Congressional Globe,* Vol. 18, 30 Congress, First Session, Washington, Blair & Rives, 1848.

3. *The Official Correspondence of James S. Calhoun while Indian Agent at Santa Fe and Superintendent of Indian Affairs in New Mexico 1849-52,* A. H. Abel, ed., Washington, 1915.

4. Fletcher M. Green, "James S. Calhoun: Pioneer Georgia Leader and First Governor of New Mexico," *The Georgia Historical Quarterly,* Dec. 1955.

5. *The Official Correspondence of James S. Calhoun, op. cit.* (letter from Jas. H. Dunn, uncle of the child, to H. H. Stuart, Secy. of Interior, Oct. 9, 1850).

6. *Ibid.*

7. In spite of strenuous efforts by Calhoun and his agents, and many other persons, the fate of Mrs. J. M. White and her daughter remains a mystery to this day.

8. *The Official Correspondence of James S. Calhoun, op. cit.*

9. *Territorial Papers of the U.S. Department of State,* New Mexico, March 3, 1851—Dec. 8, 1860, National Archives, Washington.

10. *The Official Correspondence of James S. Calhoun, op. cit.* (March 22, 1851).

11. *Ibid* (March 29, 1851).

12. *Ibid* (March 31, 1851).

13. *Territorial Papers of the U.S. Department of State, op. cit.*

14. *Ibid.*

15. *Ibid.*

16. *Ibid.*

17. *Ibid.*

18. *The Official Correspondence of James S. Calhoun, op. cit.*

19. Not until 1857 was the office of superintendent of Indian affairs separated from that of governor.

20. *The Official Correspondence of James S. Calhoun, op. cit.*

21. Lena Dargan, "James S. Calhoun in New Mexico," (unpublished Master's thesis, University of New Mexico, 1932).

22. *The Official Correspondence of James S. Calhoun, op. cit.*

23. *Ibid.*

24. On Nov. 7, 1849, in a far-seeing summary of the situation, Calhoun said: "Economy urges the adoption of a new policy—the old one should not be continued. Every Indian difficulty in this territory should be settled, and fixed, during the ensuing twelve months, and I say, after due reflection, if the present course of policy, or management is to be continued, our troubles and difficulties with these Indians, will not end in twelve years. Posts must be established—the country must be thoroughly scoured and explored; commerce with the Indians must be restricted; and they should be required to remain within certain fixed and well defined limits, under pain and penalties, that would secure the end, or prevent its repetition." (*The Official Correspondence of James S. Calhoun, op. cit.*)

25. Statement by Dr. W. L. Campbell, Vice-President, Missouri Historical Society, Santa Fe, June 30, 1906.

WILLIAM CARR LANE

TWO

Bold and Brave

WILLIAM CARR LANE

1852-53

WHEN WILLIAM CARR LANE ACCEPTED APPOINT-
MENT as the second territorial governor of New
Mexico from President Millard Fillmore in
1852, he had already enjoyed a full career in St. Louis. He
was one of that city's leading citizens—a respected surgeon,
and the first mayor.

Doctor Lane previously had declined a seat in the
United States Senate. Yet, when the offer came for appointment to a post as a frontier governor, he accepted immediately, and eagerly.

The appointment came at a critical time in the personal life of Doctor Lane. He wanted to leave St. Louis, his
medical practice, his friends, even his beloved wife Mary,
his two daughters and his grandchildren.

Personal tragedy had caused the respected St. Louis
surgeon to throw over his career and to seek a change. He
hoped that his duties in New Mexico would enable him to
recover from the grief he had suffered since the death of his
son. Victor "Ralph" Carr Lane died in 1846 at the age of
sixteen. Had it not been for Doctor Lane's prolonged grief,
he might have refused the New Mexico appointment.[1]

Lane's education and experience made him an excellent choice for governor of New Mexico. Born on a farm near Brownville, Pennsylvania, in 1789, one of eleven children, he had been educated at Jefferson College at Chambersburg and at Dickinson College at Carlisle. Lane had studied medicine in Louisville, Kentucky, and at the University of Pennsylvania. He took up the practice of medicine in Missouri, and served in the legislature of Missouri in 1826, 1830 and 1832. In 1832, he was elected first mayor of St. Louis, and was re-elected eight times.[2] Historian Ralph E. Twitchell commented on his popularity: "He was offered and could have at any time been elected to the United States Senate over Colonel Thomas H. Benton . . . but Doctor Lane positively declined the distinguished position."[3]

Through the many letters he wrote to his family, a picture emerges of New Mexico a hundred years ago—its problems, its people and its governor. Lane wrote to his daughter while he was traveling the Santa Fe Trail en route to New Mexico: "It is worth a journey of 300 or 400 miles to see a herd of probably 100,000 buffalo; and dare say, I saw that number, and probably double that number in continuous herd. . . ."[4]

Lane reached Santa Fe on September 9, 1852, forty days after leaving St. Louis. A large group of citizens, led by John Greiner, secretary of the territory, greeted him nine miles above Santa Fe. Lane wrote: "Many citizens in carriage and mounted . . . joined the escort with great spirit, and, in this way, I entered the city and drove to the Palace or the Plaza, amidst a thundering salute from Colonel Horace Brooks' Company of Artillery."[5]

Four days later, on September 13, 1852, he was sworn in as the second territorial governor. He wrote in his diary:

At twelve noon was inaugurated in front of the Governor's House, the crowd being too great for any of the
rooms. The ceremony was opened by a prayer from Mr.
Smith. [Reverend Louis Smith, Baptist missionary] I then
read my speech.[6]

He began his inaugural address:

Gentlemen, I have come amongst you with two ob-
jects in view; namely, to employ my time honorably to myself, and usefully to the people of this Territory. I have no
other object whatever in view, and if I fail in these, I fail
entirely. . . . I have not come to improve my own private
fortune, nor that of any other person, nor to advance the
political views of any individual or party. I am unpledged,
and perfectly free to do whatever I may judge to be for
the best, without being biased by party, by national or by
religious prepossessions.
. . . The task before us, public and private, now is
to build up that which has been torn down by revolutions,
to harmonize conflicting laws, and to reconcile conven-
tionalities in social life, so as to produce civity of action
and goodwill throughout the land.[7]

Of his first days in New Mexico, he confessed to Mary:

I had the blues dreadfully, at first, and would have
made an immediate retreat, if I could have done it with
honor; but I am becoming more reconciled.
Your agony, when we parted, still wrings my heart.
What would I not give to have my six little ones here.
At church today, the missionary prayed for my family, and
it was fortunate for me that my face was to the wall, for I
could not help shedding tears.[8]

The new governor had difficulty almost immediately
with the military commander, Col. E. V. Sumner—a diffi-

culty not new to the territory, and one that was to continue
during Lane's entire service in New Mexico. Colonel Sumner had been acting governor in New Mexico from the departure of Gov. James S. Calhoun until the arrival of Doctor Lane. Sumner resented losing the authority he had enjoyed and showed his feelings. He reprimanded one of his
officers, Col. Horace Brooks, for firing a salute in the plaza
at the inauguration of Governor Lane. Sumner wished
"Colonel Brooks to consider his force only as a guard for
the United States military stores." He also desired "it to be
distinctly understood that the civil government in New
Mexico is not to depend in any way upon the military authority."[9]

This first act of discord was followed by others that
continued to separate the two New Mexico leaders until
their climactic clash over the use of United States troops in
a threatened encounter with Mexico.

Upon the arrival of Governor Lane, Colonel Sumner
ordered the American flag, the only emblem of the United
States government in Santa Fe, taken down. This flag had
flown over the plaza since Kearny's conquest of New Mexico in 1846. When Governor Lane courteously applied for
the flag, Colonel Sumner replied that he was not authorized
to furnish the governor with government stores.[10] This ex-
change nearly led to a duel between the two. Lane, a tall,
athletic, red-haired man, was high-tempered and did not receive the rebuff kindly. Months later, Governor Lane actually challenged Sumner to a duel when Sumner refused to
use five hundred volunteers to suppress the Navajos. Sumner declined to fight the duel.[11]

Governor Lane blamed Sumner for conditions existing in New Mexico upon his arrival:

Never was an executive officer in a more pitiable plight than I was at this time. I was an utter stranger to my official duties, without having any competent legal advisor, and with scarcely an official document on file to direct or assist my official actions . . . not a cent of money on hand, or known to be subject to the draft of the governor . . . not a cent in the city, county or territorial treasuries, and no credit for the country . . . nor was there a single company of militia organized in the whole territory, nor a single musket within the reach of a volunteer, should there be an offer of service by anyone; and you, Colonel Sumner, must have been, from your official position, duly informed of these things.[12]

In his letters, Governor Lane did not trouble Mary with accounts of the larger problems facing him. He wrote to her:

You ask how I like playing governor. Well, only so, so,—but better than I did at first. . . . You hear, or read, 'governor', or *'governador'*, every five minutes—besides getting at least fifty embraces, from Indians and sometimes from Mexicans daily . . . the custom does not suit the taste of one of us. . . . The 'otium' of which you speak consists of an incessant round of business appointments from eight in the morning, until ten or eleven at night. . . . I still lead a sort of hermit-life. The people are not sociable, or perhaps the fault is in me. But we are, nevertheless, very friendly. . . . I am too busy to be lonesome. . . . Many serious official difficulties have opposed me, thus far; but I met them, as you would wish your husband to meet a high duty.[13]

He enjoyed telling Mary of everyday events:

I am in luck. The officers at Fort Union have just sent me some venison, some antelope venison, and a wild turkey

. . . we have fine beets and beans, and some parsnips and
excellent onions, and some dried peaches; but no butter,
and no milk. We have, however, fresh eggs. Then we have
some starved chickens; they are so miserably poor that I
wonder how they can muster up spirits to crow as much
as they do.[14]

In addition to military trouble, Governor Lane's administration was plagued with Indian problems. Early in
his term, he signed treaties with the Indians, agreeing to
supply them with corn, salt, beef and breeding animals.
Lane agreed to furnish the Apaches food for five years—at
least that was the understanding of the Apaches. He moved
the Jicarillas from the north to farms on the Rio Puerco.
He advanced funds to members of the Mimbres Apache
group. Lane spent all the money possible—$20,000—on the
Indians.[15] This course of action was less costly than fighting
them, but the treaties he negotiated had to be approved by
the United States Senate. They were not approved. When
the Apaches felt that the treaties had been broken, they became bitter and unmanageable, stealing and killing to even
the bargain.

Governor Lane administered justice quickly and fairly.
He handled Indian disputes by searching for all the details.
The murder of an Apache by an American in Las Vegas
was handled effectively. John Ward, Indian secretary in
Santa Fe, noted on November 19:

Information has been received at this office that an
American at the sawmill . . . near Las Vegas, had shot an
Apache Indian and badly wounded two others: the gover-
nor, upon receiving the above information, consulted with
Mr. Greiner, secretary, and requested him to proceed to
Las Vegas and have the matter investigated—the governor

also requested Mr. Greiner to see the Indians and to spare no means in order to have them pacified and the injured families rewarded as much as possible, in order to prevent any trouble hereafter by the Indians trying to revenge themselves.[16]

Ten days later, a diary entry states:

> Mr. Greiner arrived last evening from Las Vegas and states all the Indian difficulties settled.[17]

Restless, even though a busy administrator, Governor Lane traveled continually. He visited seven of the territorial counties, now numbering nine, leaving Santa Fe only three weeks after his inauguration. He made a journey on horseback to Taos in the middle of January, a rugged undertaking. During his travels, Lane became thoroughly enamored of the country and the people. He wrote to his wife:

> Indeed, this climate is so excellent, Mary, that I verily believe that I could reasonably calculate upon a considerable extension of my lease of life—were I to remain in the country.
> . . . the mountains . . . are covered with snow (in Santa Fe) from summit to base . . . on the plain there is no appearance of winter. These contrasts are, to my view, strikingly beautiful.[18]

He loved the people of New Mexico. Of them, he said:

> I do not advise them to change any of their beneficial or praiseworthy customs, nor do I advise them to forget their parent stock, and the proud recollections that cluster around Castillian history. I do not advise them to disuse their beautiful language, to lay aside their dignified manners and punctilious attention to the proprieties of social life, and I sincerely hope the profound deference that is

now paid to age by the young will undergo no change. . . .
True it is that the Mexican people have been always noted
for their distinguished manners and Christian customs. It
is only to be regretted to see that some of their good usages
are disappearing little by little before what is called progress in our day.[19]

Later, Doctor Lane wrote Mary again of his affection
for the people. When he was campaigning to represent New
Mexico in Congress, the citizens of Las Vegas told him not
to expect support: "They say they have no personal objec-
tion to me, but that they are determined to elect one of their
own race—God bless them."[20]

The Legislature met December 7, 1852. Lane had earlier expressed concern to Mary:

> . . . a new set of troubles come up. The Legislature
> will convene, and I will have one House in one adjoining
> room, and the other House, in the adjoining room, with-
> out understanding a word that is said in either. This trial
> of patience will endure for 40 days . . . ominous period.
> It will not be a fact, but a penance, and I hope it will
> yield some good fruits.[21]

Governor Lane in his first legislative address listed the
liabilities and assets of New Mexico:

> It cannot be denied that the first aspect of things in
> this Territory is discouraging.
> We are distant from the states . . . your people are
> so badly armed that they cannot protect their own property
> from depredation. . . .
> Your highways are in bad condition, and the school-
> master is rarely seen amongst you. . . .
> The country is run over with red and white thieves
> and robbers. Your prisons are insecure.

Your revenue laws are so defective that sufficient funds are not provided for the ordinary purposes of government.

These discouragements would be appalling were it not evident to every reflecting mind that all these difficulties are either temporary or removable by proper exertions. . . .

Let us now bring into view some of the sources from which public and private prosperity may be expected to flow. Your country is one of the healthiest on the globe . . . your tillable land may be increased, perhaps more than a thousand fold, by improved *acequias* and by *tanques* . . . your facilities for stock-raising are unequalled. . . . From public and private necessity, this continent must soon be crossed, from east to west, by railroad and telegraph lines, and, in all probabilities, one or more of these railroads and telegraphic lines will traverse New Mexico. . . .

He recommended the repeal of the law which authorized licensing of gambling houses, and commented on the official bilinguality of the legislature:

I leave the question whether the laws should be passed in English or Spanish to be decided by you alone. Adopt whichever language you please and I shall be content, but I protest, in advance, against the laws being passed, as heretofore, in duplicate.[22]

It is interesting, but not surprising, to note that the affairs of New Mexico, during the entire territorial period, were conducted both in Spanish and in English. The legislature did not take Governor Lane's suggestion that one of the languages be dropped.

Ballots, legislative bills and messages, state documents of all kinds, were printed in English and in Spanish and the services of translators were available at all territorial legislative sessions. Many of the governors depended upon the services of bilingual secretaries or other trusted persons for the writing of speeches and the daily conduct of business.

Even today, bilinguality is the practice in some state business, as a matter of courtesy and when it seems to be necessary. In political campaigns, both languages are used extensively.

The most far-reaching act of Governor Lane's administration was his attempt to settle the U.S.–Mexican boundary dispute even though he lacked authority from the Federal government to do so.

Because the maps were inaccurate, the southern boundary of New Mexico was in dispute. The location of the boundary was the subject of much official discussion. Emotions ran high and, finally, some Mesilla Valley citizens petitioned the governor for protection from Mexico.[23]

While officials in Washington continued to discuss the situation, Governor Lane took swift action. He went to Doña Ana and there, on March 13, 1853, issued a proclamation taking possession of the disputed territory. The proclamation said, in part:

> . . . I, William Carr Lane, Governor of the Territory of New Mexico (upon my own official responsibility and without orders from the cabinet at Washington) do hereby, in behalf of the United States, retake possession of the said disputed territory to be held provisionally by the United States until the question of boundary shall be determined by the United States and the Mexican Republic. . . .[24]

Lane was prepared to use force, if necessary, to take and to hold the disputed territory. He had written to his wife on February 15:

> Be not surprised if I should take possession of the disputed territory, which I dare say I will find to be without adequate protection, against internal and external violence . . . if duty calls upon me to occupy and protect this country, provisionally, until the line shall be definitely established, I will do it. . . .[25]

Excitement ran high in both countries. President Santa Anna ordered Gen. Angel Trias, governor of Chihuahua, to march Mexican troops into the Mesilla Valley and to resist all U.S. attempts to take possession. Lane prepared to fight. When Colonel Sumner refused the use of federal troops, Lane made plans to use volunteer New Mexico and Texas troops against Mexico.

Alfred Conkling, United States Minister to Mexico, bitterly protested Lane's action. Lane replied that he had been "appointed Governor of all New Mexico, and not a part."[26]

In Washington, Secretary of State W. L. Marcy justified Lane's claim to the disputed region, but he did not approve forceful action.

Public opinion in the United States was expressed by the New Orleans *Picayune Report*:

> It certainly is not for the Governor of a territory of the United States to anticipate the decision of the federal government of a question of so delicate a nature as the drawing of a boundary line between that territory and a foreign state.[27]

In the end, the dispute was settled without bloodshed. Just when another Mexican War appeared inevitable, James Gadsden, as agent for the United States, purchased the disputed area, and additional land, for ten million dollars.

Governor Lane's plan to take the Mesilla Valley by force had enabled the United States to bargain from a position of strength. Historian Paul Garber has commented: "Lane did not take possession of the Mesilla Valley, as he had accomplished his intention of forcing the federal government to take action."[28]

During the summer of 1853, Governor Lane resigned as governor, desiring to represent New Mexico in Washington. He filed as a candidate for Congressional delegate for the election of September 5, 1853. He campaigned vigorously, but was defeated by Jose Manuel Gallegos by 445 votes, 4,971 to 4,526. He contested the election, but, when all the illegal ballots were thrown out, he still lost by 539 votes, 2,806 to 2,267.[29] Lane appealed to Congress. If Indian ballots were counted, he was the winner. Congress decided against the Indians' right to vote and, thereby, against Lane. He returned to St. Louis. Ten years later, in 1863, he died.

Though his administration was short, Lane had accomplished much in New Mexico. He had been instrumental in saving the Mesilla Valley for New Mexico and the United States. By his affection for the people and by his travel among them, he added stature to the governorship. His kindness, mature understanding and appreciation for things New Mexican won friendship and respect for the governor's office.

He had been successful in obtaining legislation to limit gambling and to increase revenues to the counties and to the state. He obtained laws providing procedures for removing officials from office, and for auditing their accounts. The legislature provided penalties for anyone bartering, selling or giving away spirituous liquor to Indians.

Praise for Lane, during his administration and after his retirement, came from many sources. During his term in office, a statement appeared in the Baltimore *American*: "There is a bold and brave public servant in the administration of national interests at present in New Mexico."[30]

As he sought to serve New Mexico, so, too, did New Mexico do much for Governor Lane. After ten months in the territory, he reflected in a letter to Mary on the tragedy which brought him to New Mexico:

> I cannot say these 10 months have been blessed . . . [but] the agonizing associations connected with St. Louis have not harassed me. Oh, God, I give thee thanks for this merciful dispensation of Thy providence.[31]

In the territory, there was rising pressure for statehood, and pressing problems—some old, some new— awaited solution.

NOTES

1. Letter from William G. B. Carson, great-grandson of William Carr Lane, May 3, 1957.

2. Stella M. Drumm, *Letters of William Carr Lane 1819-1831—Glimpses of the Past,* ed. by Missouri Historical Society, St. Louis, Jefferson, 1940.

3. Ralph E. Twitchell, "Historical Sketch of Governor William Carr Lane," *Historical Society of New Mexico, No. 4,* Santa Fe, 1917.

4. R. P. Bieber, "Letters of William Carr Lane 1852-1854," *The New Mexico Historical Review,* v. III, April 1928.

5. *Ibid.*

6. *Ibid.*

7. *Territorial Papers of the U.S. Department of State,* New Mexico, March 3, 1851—Dec. 8, 1860, National Archives, Washington.

8. Personal letters of William Carr Lane, from the collection of William G. B. Carson (unpublished).

9. Twitchell, *op. cit.*

10. *Ibid.*

11. J. Manuel Espinosa, "Memoir of a Kentuckian in New Mexico," *The New Mexico Historical Review,* v. XIII, January 1938.

12. Twitchell, *op. cit.*

13. Bieber, *op. cit.*

14. *Ibid.*

15. A. B. Bender, "Frontier Defense in the Territory of New Mexico, 1846-1853," *The New Mexico Historical Review,* v. IX, July 1934.

16. A. H. Abel, "Indian Affairs in New Mexico under the Administration of William Carr Lane" (from the journal of John Ward), *The New Mexico Historical Review,* v. XVI, July 1941.

17. *Ibid.*

18. Bieber, *op. cit.*

19. *Territorial Papers of the U.S. Department of State, op. cit.*

20. Bieber, *op. cit.*

21. *Ibid.*

22. *Territorial Papers of the U.S. Department of State, op. cit.*

23. Loomis Morton Gannaway, *New Mexico and the Sectional Controversy, 1846-1861,* Albuquerque, Univ. of New Mexico, 1944.

24. Ralph E. Twitchell, *The Leading Facts of New Mexican History,* Vol. II, Cedar Rapids, Torch, 1912.

25. Personal letters of William Carr Lane from the collection of William G. B. Carson.

26. Paul Neff Garber, *The Gadsden Treaty*, Philadelphia, Univ. of Penn., 1923.

27. Abel, *op. cit.*

28. Garber, *op. cit.*

29. *Territorial Papers of U.S. Department of State, op. cit.*

30. Abel, *op. cit.*

31. Bieber, *op. cit.*

DAVID MERIWETHER

THREE

Trouble Shooter

DAVID MERIWETHER

1853-57

A T NINETEEN, DAVID MERIWETHER, A KENTUCKY FARM boy and member of an ill-fated trading party to New Mexico, was imprisoned in irons for a month in the dungeon at the west end of the Palace of the Governors in Santa Fe. He was held by the Mexican government, accused of being a spy for the United States.

Thirty-four years later, on August 8, 1853, the same tall, sharp-featured David Meriwether, now fifty-three, stood in the council room of the Palace and took the oath of office as governor of the Territory of New Mexico.

On the very day of his inauguration, the roof of the cell where he had been shackled thirty-four years earlier fell in. The people of Santa Fe, and probably the new governor, took it as a favorable omen.

Between the year of his release from prison, when he made his way back to the East, and the time of his return as governor, David Meriwether had become a successful farmer, father of seven children, a rough-and-tumble politician, and an important office-holder in Kentucky, where he served many years in the Kentucky General Assembly.[1]

In 1852, he was appointed United States senator to fill the vacancy caused by the death of Henry Clay. The following year, President Franklin Pierce appointed him governor of New Mexico, with special instructions to improve relations with Mexico, which had deteriorated over the question of the disputed Mesilla territory, which Meriwether's predecessor, William Carr Lane, had threatened to take by force.

In his first report to United States Secretary of State William C. Marcy, August 13, 1853, Meriwether commented on the dispute:

> I have immediately applied myself to the discharge of the special duties assigned to me. . . . From the best information I can gather, the Mexican government has at present about thirty troops stationed upon the disputed territory. . . .[2]

In November 1853, an Indian chief was murdered in the area by a citizen of the Mesilla Valley. The Indians, trusting in the justice of the white man, appealed to the new governor for the arrest of the known murderer, who was under the protection of Mexico.

Meriwether, undecided on a course of action, wrote to Marcy in Washington, November 14, 1853, for instructions that were to take months in coming:

> . . . I am at a loss how to act. . . . Should I demand from the Governor of Chihuahua the delivery of this criminal? I am inclined to the belief that he would be surrendered, but such an act on my part might be constructed into an acknowledgment of their possession. . . . Should I attempt a forcible arrest within the disputed territory, I

am confident that I could succeed, but this might precipi-
tate matters more than is desirable to the government at
Washington. Hence, I refer the matter to the department
for instructions.[3]

Meriwether was under definite instructions from Secretary of State Marcy to "abstain from taking forcible possession of the tract [Mesilla Valley] even if on your arrival in
New Mexico you find it held adversely to the claims of the
United States by Mexico or the authorities of Chihuahua."[4]
Governor Meriwether attempted to follow literally each in-
struction from Washington as he received it.

A year later, December 5, 1854, he reported to the territorial Legislature:

> I am happy to inform you that the long disputed ques-
> tion of boundary between this Territory and the State of
> Chihuahua has been amicably settled by the governments
> of the United States and Mexico [The Gadsden Purchase].[5]

Meanwhile, the criminal who killed the Indian had
been tried and convicted of murder by the United States
authorities. The patience of the new governor was bringing results.

Governor Meriwether sought to build better understanding with the governor of Chihuahua by stopping traffic
in Mexican children. En route to New Mexico for his inauguration, Meriwether had come upon two Mexican girls
who had escaped from their Indian captors, and he returned
them to the governor of Chihuahua. Meriwether wrote to
the governor:

> In this act, it is hoped that your Excellency and the
> government of Mexico will find evidence of the disposition,

on the part of the government of the United States, strictly to comply with its obligations as well as the dictates of humanity.[6]

James Gadsden, minister to Mexico, wrote Meriwether in October 1853:

> A more serious charge has been made that the Garrison . . . which I presume to be Fort Webster, encourages or permits an intercourse with the Indians and that they purchase from them the Mexican prisoners which the Indians bring in. . . .[7]

Investigation revealed that the officers and one Indian agent at Fort Webster had purchased Mexican children from the Indians. The buyers explained that they were attempting to help the captives by returning them to Mexico as soon as their work repaid the purchase price. Meriwether wrote the Indian agent: "Such a traffic can never be tolerated, as this would be to offer a premium to the Indians for the capture of others."[8]

Besides questions of disputed territory and slave traffic, Meriwether faced other problems during his four years as governor. There were Indian uprisings, the need to construct a capitol and a penitentiary, and the immediate necessity of dealing with legislative matters.

Meriwether asked the first legislative session, December 5, 1853, for "a sufficient amount of revenue to defray the cost of an economical administration of government," reporting that the receipts for the year ending November 15, 1853, were $3,886, with payments of $3,899. He listed the old debts of the territory, showing a deficit of $7,309. He recommended prohibition of gambling, revision of the election

laws, and revision of the penal code. He offered an example
of the need for the latter:

> . . . I take the liberty of stating the fact of my having
> exercised the pardoning power . . . in favor of an indi-
> vidual who had been incarcerated in one of the jails of the
> Territory for a period of five years, in consequence of his
> inability to pay a fine of fifty dollars.[9]

The legislature followed many of the governor's recommendations, including the election and penal code revisions
and the elimination of gambling.

During the first legislative session, Governor Meriwether became involved in a bitter legislative fight. The
secretary of the territory was authorized to let a lucrative
contract for public printing. The governor suggested to the
secretary that the two legislative Houses, the Council and the
House of Representatives, select the public printer, the members of both Houses voting together. A resolution to this
effect was introduced and passed in the Council. The House
failed to take action.

The Council then took separate action, selecting the
Santa Fe *Gazette* as the public printer. This angered the
House, for many of the members of the House had differed
strongly with the position taken by the *Gazette* in the Congressional election held September 18, 1853. The House, by
its own action, selected another printer, S. M. Baird. Yet,
three days before the adjournment of the legislature, on
Monday, January 30, 1854, the House passed, by a one-vote
majority, on second (but not final) passage, the Council's
resolution on printing. The House then adjourned until
nine o'clock the next morning. Hoping to prevent final action
on the measure, ten members of the House minority who

opposed the awarding of the printing contract to the *Gazette*
met prior to session time and adjourned the legislature until
Thursday evening, three hours after the legal adjournment
time.

The Santa Fe *Gazette* was highly critical of their action:
"To make their course the ranker treason, they even took
into consideration the propriety of raising a mob and turning the members out of the House by force, but this proposi-
tion . . . was voted down."

The House continued about its business in spite of the
action of the dissatisfied minority. Two days later, the rebels
sent a resolution to the President of the United States:

> We, the undersigned, members of said House . . .
> most solemnly protest against all acts (The Public Printing
> Act) done by the said majority, in a legislative capacity
> during said adjournment as null and void.[10]

The rebels also attempted to discredit the secretary of
the territory, but failed. Governor Meriwether defended the
secretary in a letter to Secretary of State Marcy, February 22,
1854:

> I am in no way implicated, and, hence, think I can
> give an impartial statement of fact. . . . I would not have
> troubled you with the communication but for the fact that
> copies of these papers are to be sent to the President and
> both houses of Congress, and I desired the truth should be
> known before any action is had on them.
> Mr. Misservy, the Secretary of the Territory, on in-
> structions from the Treasury Department was authorized
> to make a contract for public printing for the Legislative
> Assembly. . . . In conclusion, allow me to say, that after a
> careful review of the act of the Secretary, and a full knowl-

edge of all the facts connected with the transaction, I am unable to see wherein he deserves censure.[11]

In his address to the joint session of this same legislature on December 5, 1853, Governor Meriwether had been concerned about education: " . . . Unless the public mind be enlightened, no people can ever attain a very high degree of prosperity and happiness."

A year later, Governor Meriwether again discussed education before the legislature: "There is no subject whatever of more vital importance than this. . . . " He was finally successful in obtaining a law stipulating financing for public education:

> Every male, whose property does not exceed $250 in value, shall pay an annual tax of one dollar, and an additional dollar tax on each $1,000 worth of property, up to a maximum of $50.

The legislature, however, put a joker in the bill:

> . . . Provided, that the law shall not be in force in the counties of Taos, Rio Arriba, Santa Ana, and Socorro, but it shall be submitted to the approval of a majority of the voters in each one of said counties . . . when the Governor shall have been informed of the counties in which a majority has been given in favor of the law, he shall announce the same by proclamation, declaring that this law is in full force and vigor, and where a majority is not had, this law shall not be in force.[12]

The election was held March 31, 1856. There were 37 votes for and 5,016 against public education. The next legislature repealed the law.

W. W. H. Davis in 1856 reported on the problem of
public education in New Mexico:

> This great enmity to schools and intelligence can only
> be accounted for as follows: that the people are so far sunk
> in ignorance that they are not really capable of judging the
> advantages of education. From this result the cause of edu-
> cation has but little to hope for from the popular will, and
> the verdict shows that the people love darkness rather than
> light.[13]

Governor Meriwether, although bitter in clashes with
opposing officials, could be wise and understanding. The
House, during the first legislative session, desired him to fire
the translator, but he counseled:

> Now one of our great conservative principles of our
> happy form of government is to be found in its division
> into three separate departments . . . and that provision
> which prohibits one department from exercising any of
> the powers properly belonging to another.[14]

In a firm but friendly letter of October 29, 1853, he
instructed a justice of the peace to enforce the law:

> Sir, I am informed that there are persons in the village
> of Pecos who sell spirituous liquors to the Indians . . .
> and it is your duty to prevent such a practice. . . . I,
> therefore, send you a copy of the laws of this Territory in-
> tended to apply to such cases, and trust that this law will
> be rigidly enforced on all occasions of its violation.[15]

In February 1854, Governor Meriwether returned to
Kentucky to attend to private business and to bring his wife
and family to Santa Fe. Shortly after he left the territory, the

Indians went on the warpath, and Meriwether hastened back to face this problem, leaving his family to join him later.

He was plagued all during 1854 and 1855 with Indian uprisings, Indian treaties, and trouble with Indian agents— including Christopher "Kit" Carson, who was already on his way to fame. The basic problem was reported to Secretary Marcy September 1, 1854:

> It will be found that my predecessor, on the part of the United States, contracted with the Indians that they . . . should be supplied with food, to consist of corn, beef, and salt, for that current year [1853] and the year 1854, and to give them a reasonable amount of food for three years thereafter. . . .
>
> They ask how it was that the former Father could satisfy them with food . . . whilst their present Father could not. When I say to them that I have no money to purchase presents and provisions with, their reply is, how did their former Father get money for this purpose.[16]

Governor Meriwether understood the plight of the Indians; they had to be fed until they could plant and harvest crops, or they had to live off the settlements.

In a legislative address of December 1854, Meriwether spoke of Indians: " . . . I regret extremely to inform you that since the adjournment of the last legislative assembly, our citizens have suffered much from depredations committed by the Indians."[17]

To deal with the Indians, Meriwether believed that the government must either feed and clothe them to a certain extent or chastise them in a decisive manner. His position was weakened by the fact that, although his predecessor had made liberal treaties with the Jicarilla and the Gila Apaches, the Senate had failed to ratify the treaties.

In July 1854, Congress appropriated $30,000 to defer the cost of making treaties with the Apache, Utah and Navajo Indians. Governor Meriwether was appointed special commissioner to carry out the terms of the act. W. W. H. Davis, secretary to the governor reported: "Gov. Meriwether has been appointed sole commissioner to make treaties with the various Indian tribes of the Territory."[18]

During 1854, the Indians declared, "they will war with the United States as long as any of them are left alive or until the white population are driven from the Territory."[19] The Indians, feeling the government had dealt with them in bad faith, "subsisted themselves during the next year at the expense of the settlements which were reported to have suffered a loss of several lives and nearly $100,000 worth of property."[20] The villages and settlements organized themselves to be ready to repulse the invasions of the Indians.

The Pueblo Indians, however, continued to cooperate with the government. In 1854, Governor Meriwether went to Taos and aided in vaccinating the Taos children.

In June, 1855, Meriwether made a treaty with the Mescalero Apaches after a campaign in which the Indians were completely defeated. The treaty provided for a reservation in the vicinity of Fort Stanton and the present Mescalero Indian reservation. Meriwether also made a treaty with the Mimbres Apaches.

The Apache problem being resolved, Meriwether, with four others and without military escort, set out in July, 1855, to meet with the Navajos. In the party with the governor were his son, his secretary, and two servants. They set up headquarters in the heart of the Navajo country, at Laguna Negra, fourteen miles from Fort Defiance.

W. W. H. Davis told of the interview between the governor of New Mexico and the Navajo governor, Manuelito:

> The governor . . . told the Indians that he had been sent there by their Great Father in Washington to hold a talk and make a treaty with them. [The Navajos] were to be confined within a certain district of country . . . for which they would receive annuities in goods for some 20 years.

Another condition was that the Navajos were to live in peace and cultivate the soil.

The following morning, Governor Manuelito replied that "they were in the habit of going to the mountain of Polonia, outside the [proposed] reservation, to worship the spirits of their fathers, and that some were adverse to giving up this sacred spot." Governor Meriwether explained that the sacred spot would remain in their reservation. The Indians were satisfied and signed the treaty.[21]

By the fall of 1855, it was reported to the legislature that "we are at peace with the Indian tribes of the Territory."[22] But New Mexico citizens were not pleased with the land given to the Indians. Utah Indian Agent Diego Archuleta complained, "The treaties negotiated by Gov. and Supt. Meriwether were in direct violation of the rights of individuals, because the selections of the reservations were not only upon private grants, but also so proximate to the settlements" that great injustice was done.[23]

Another Indian agent, Michael Steck, claimed that the land given to the Mescalero Indians "is in the centre of the most valuable portion of New Mexico." The citizens were so irate about the treaties that a diary of 1855 noted: "Last night the Governor of the Territory was hung in effigy to the flag staff in the main plaza. Cause: his course taken with the Indians."[24]

The Indian treaties negotiated by Governor Meriwether, like those negotiated by his predecessor, were not approved by the United States Senate. The failure of the Senate to ratify the treaties eventually contributed to greater Indian troubles in New Mexico.

Governor Meriwether, as superintendent of Indian affairs, differed with Taos Indian Agent Kit Carson. Mr. Carson, agent for seven and one-half years, could not read or write. Carson's illiteracy probably caused the series of differences with Meriwether, who was a stickler for exact reports. Governor Meriwether did, however, recognize the difficult job assigned to Kit Carson—handling the Mohuache Utahs, who, Meriwether admitted, were "probably the most difficult Indians to manage within the Territory," and the Jicarilla Apaches of whom Meriwether said, "No other single band of Indians . . . have caused so much trouble and annoyance to the people of this Territory . . . whenever there is any mischief brewing [they] invariably have a hand in it."[25]

When Kit Carson sent his first report to the governor, Meriwether noted: "Mr. Carson does not inform me what Indians committed these depredations . . . It is to be regretted that Agent Carson did not ascertain from the prisoners what Indians they were."[26]

Carson's financial reports were usually returned by Meriwether for correction, and some were submitted to Washington for special audit. The governor reproved Carson, September 29, 1855, with a typical letter:

> After your departure from Santa Fe, I discovered some errors in your accounts which I beg leave to notice. . . . I

have approved your voucher for Mr. Master [John Master]
as interpreter, but I deem it my duty to inform you that I
cannot do so again.[27]

To George Manypenny, Indian commissioner in Washington, Meriwether had written on September 1:

> I am informed and believe that John Master, the in-
> terpreter employed by Agent Carson, can neither speak the
> Indian or Spanish language as well as Mr. Carson, himself,
> but that he is a discharged soldier who is employed for his
> clerical service.[28]

On another occasion, Meriwether wrote to Manypenny:

> I see no objection to his [Carson's] accounts for this
> quarter [June 30, 1856] so far as the expenditures belong
> properly to the quarters, but they are so blended with items
> belonging to previous years that is is impossible for me to
> understand them.[29]

Kit Carson struck back at Meriwether. He declined to
help the governor with problems in the Taos pueblo. When
Governor Meriwether appointed Capt. Ceran St. Vrain commander of the volunteers, Carson observed: "It was the only
appointment of the Governor that met the approbation of
the people. Many were surprised at the sound judgment in
making such a noble choice."[30]

Meriwether's secretary, W. W. H. Davis, described Kit
Carson as a "small-sized, modest-looking person . . . about
five feet eight inches in height, rather heavy-set and a little
bow-legged . . . he is a mild, pleasant man in conversation,
with a voice almost as soft as that of a woman."[31]

During much of his term, Governor Meriwether engaged in controversy with officials and citizens about the

building of a capitol and a penitentiary. As Congress had appropriated $20,000 for the erection of a capitol in 1850, work was under way when Meriwether was inaugurated.

In May 1853, Congress appropriated $20,000 for a penitentiary for the territory. The Secretary of the United States Treasury, James Guthrie, authorized Governor Meriwether to select a site for the penitentiary. The diary of Meriwether's secretary records:

> On a vacant lot north of the Palace, and near the American Cemetery, a new statehouse is in course of erection . . . which, when completed, will make a handsome and imposing edifice, and of which the Territory stands in great need. Nearby, and a little to the northeast, is the site of the new penitentiary, also in course of erection. Such an institution is badly wanted, and the country abounds with admirable subjects for it.[32]

After he had been in New Mexico only two months, Meriwether decided to remove the building commissioners, and wrote Secretary James Guthrie on October 28, 1853: "Should you discover anything improper on the part of the present commissioners or the superintendent, which I think highly probable will be the case—you may rest assured that we will have a better set before this reaches you. . . ."[33] After their removal, Governor Meriwether himself took over the work of the building commissioners.

The ousted commissioners and their friends fought back. About seventy-five citizens petitioned Guthrie, complaining that the penitentiary was being built too close to their homes. The citizens also made application for an injunction against Meriwether in the U.S. District Court.

Meriwether answered charges concerning the location of the new penitentiary:

The truth is that this thing was gotten up by persons whom it is impossible to please without surrendering the government of the Territory entirely into their hands, and particularly the disbursement of the public funds. . . . The active men in this movement are those who have been removed from, or those who have been disappointed in getting office.

It is said that nice little speculation was made out of a former appropriation, which came to the hands of the old board which it is sought to revive . . . it does not require much effort to determine where the shoe pinches.[34]

Both Washington and the Federal Court upheld Meriwether and the penitentiary was commenced.

Meriwether complained to Secretary Guthrie about the high cost of labor during the construction:

I have offered to pay $12.50 per thousand for making and laying brick, but can make no contract at that price. . . . one master carpenter and draftsman, $4.00 per day; six carpenters, one at $2.00, remainder at $2.75 a day; one master mason, $3.50 per day; one master lumberman, $2.50 per day; mortar-mixer and hod-carrier from $1.00 to $1.50 per day, and common laborers from fifty cents to $1.00 per day.[35]

Meriwether spent $72,647 on the capitol and penitentiary, but neither building was completed during his administration. The capitol was raised to one and one-half stories high, then left for many years before being completed. It was never used by the territory as a capitol building, but is now used as a federal building. The work on the penitentiary was permanently abandoned.[36]

The accomplishments of Governor Meriwether during his four years as governor of New Mexico were several. He handled a major Indian war at the beginning of his term and, in his annual report of September 30, 1856, he could report:

> Although this Territory has not remained free from Indian depredations . . . yet such occurrences have been less serious than during any preceding year since my appointment to this office. . . . The Mimbres Apaches have remained peaceable and quiet. . . . I visited [the Jicarilla Apaches] and gave them a supply of clothing, blankets, hatchets, tobacco for which they appeared very grateful. . . . I have heard of no depredations having been committed by the Navajos for several months past.[37]

During his term, the differences with Mexico were settled and the Gadsden Purchase was completed. The laws of the territory were compiled by the chief justice of the territory. Gambling was abolished.

Because of his strength of character, increased respect for the laws and ways of the United States government was established in New Mexico. Meriwether brought careful administration to the territory.

David Meriwether left New Mexico in May 1857, although his official term did not end until the following October. He returned to his farm near Louisville and again became active in Kentucky politics. He was elected to the General Assembly and, in 1859, was elected speaker of the House. He served in the assembly again during the 1880's but was eventually defeated. He was a member of eighteen different state legislatures in Kentucky.

On October 30, 1890, David Meriwether celebrated his ninetieth birthday at the home of a son, William, in Louisville. A relative wrote: "Despite the weight of years, he is still hale and hearty. His mind is clear and he delights in meeting old friends and talking over the past."[38] At the age of ninety-three, he died on his farm near Louisville on the Ohio River —the farm which had been his home, intermittently, for ninety years.

To the end of his life, David Meriwether watched with interest developments and difficulties in the territory of New Mexico which he had honorably served for four years.

NOTES

1. J. Stoddard Johnson, *Memorial History of Louisville*, v. I, (no pub.).

2. *General Records of the Department of State, Miscellaneous Letters Series,* Aug. 13, 1853—May 22, 1856, (Meriwether correspondence), National Archives, Washington.

3. *Territorial Papers of the U.S. Department of State,* New Mexico, March 3, 1851—Dec. 8, 1860, National Archives, Washington.

4. Sister Mary Loyola, "The American Occupation of New Mexico, 1821-1852," *The New Mexico Historical Review,* v. XIV, July 1939.

5. *Book of Clear Record of the Legislative Council of the Territory of New Mexico,* Dec. 1, 1851 to Jan. 30, 1856, bound ms., Santa Fe, State Records Center.

6. *Territorial Papers of the U.S. Department of State, op. cit.*

7. *Ibid.*

8. *Ibid.*

9. *Ibid.*

10. *Ibid.*

11. *Ibid.*

12. *Laws of the Territory of New Mexico, Passed by the Legislative Assembly, 1856-57,* Printed at the Office of the Democrat, 1857.

13. William Watts Hart Davis, *El Gringo: or New Mexico and her People,* Santa Fe, Rydal, 1938.

14. *Territorial Papers of the U.S. Department of State, op. cit.*

15. *Ibid.*

16. U.S. Office of Indian Affairs, *Records of the New Mexico Superintendency of Indian Affairs, 1849-80,* National Archives, Washington.

17. *Territorial Papers of the U.S. Department of State, op. cit.*

18. Davis, *op. cit.*

19. *Territorial Papers of the U.S. Department of State, op. cit.*

20. Frank D. Reeve, "The Government and the Navaho, 1846-1858," *The New Mexico Historical Review,* v. XIV, Jan. 1939.

21. U.S. Office of Indian Affairs, *Records of the New Mexico Superintendency, op. cit.*

22. Robert Daniel Hepler, "William Watts Davis in New Mexico," (unpublished Master's thesis, University of New Mexico, 1941).

23. U.S. Office of Indian Affairs, *Records of the New Mexico Superintendency, op. cit.*

24. Averam B. Bender, *The March of Empire; Frontier Defense in the Southwest, 1848-1860,* Lawrence, Univ. of Kansas, 1952.

25. Edwin Legrand Sabin, *Kit Carson Days, 1809-1868; Adventures in the Path of Empire* (rev. ed.), New York, Press of the Pioneers, 1935.

26. *Ibid.*

27. U.S. Office of Indian Affairs, *Records of the New Mexico Superintendency, op. cit.*

28. *Ibid.*

29. *General Records of the Department of State, op. cit.*

30. Christopher Carson, *Kit Carson's Own Story of His Life as Dictated to Col. and Mrs. D. C. Peters about 1856-57 and never before Published,* ed. by Blanche C. Grant, Taos, 1926.

31. Davis, *op. cit.*

32. *Ibid.*

33. *Meriwether Letters,* University of New Mexico Library, Albuquerque.

34. *Ibid.*

35. *Ibid.*

36. *Ibid.*

37. U.S. Office of Indian Affairs, *Records of the New Mexico Superintendency, op. cit.*

38. Louisa H. A. Minor, *The Meriwethers and their Connections,* Charlottesville, Univ. of Virginia, 1892.

ABRAHAM RENCHER

FOUR

Southern Patriot

ABRAHAM RENCHER

1857-61

IN 1857, ABRAHAM RENCHER, A SUCCESSFUL NORTH CARO-
LINA congressman and former minister to Portugal, actively sought an appointment to the governorship of the
territory of New Mexico. His reasons for desiring to be governor are difficult to determine. Certainly he could not have
been seeking additional political honor, for there were better positions available to him—James Buchanan, President-
elect, had offered him the post of Secretary of the Navy.[1]

Having lived in North Carolina, Washington and Switzerland, the scholarly Rencher must have known that a post
on the raw frontier would not offer the delights of these more
civilized localities. In poetry and essays, Rencher had expressed his love for Switzerland. He had written: "Switzerland is a small but romantic country, presenting every
advantage for the improvement of fancy, the cultivation of
virtue and the enjoyment of the finer feelings of the soul."[2]

Possibly his imagination was stirred by what he had
heard of New Mexico. But, whatever his reasons, he wanted
the New Mexico appointment. Many of his friends wrote
letters of recommendation to President-elect Buchanan. On

Rencher's behalf, nine North Carolina state senators petitioned Buchanan: "We cordially unite in recommending to
you our friend and fellow citizen, the Honorable Abraham
Rencher, for an appointment. . . ."[3]

"He would prefer that of governor of New Mexico. . ."
another recommendation read.[4]

He received a guarded endorsement from Miguel A.
Otero, New Mexico territorial delegate in Congress:

> I have the honor very respectfully to recommend for
> the appointment of Governor of the Territory of New
> Mexico Abraham Rencher of North Carolina, whose quali-
> fications for that office have already been made known to
> you by his own delegation.[5]

President James Buchanan appointed Abraham Rencher governor of New Mexico on August 17, 1857.

As a poet and essayist, possibly Rencher thought of New
Mexico as the unspoiled, sylvan spot that he had pictured in
imagination when he wrote:

> We fancy ourselves in a country surrounded by the
> most elegant and interesting landscape. We hear the shep-
> herd's sweetly sounding harp, and are delighted with mur-
> muring brooks as they glide along. . . . It presents to our
> imagination mountains, hills, rivers, flocks, and shepherds
> with as much simplicity and exactness as could be done by
> the most masterly hand in painting.[6]

Or he may have felt that New Mexico would welcome
a transplanted Southern gentleman, for early in 1857 the
Indians were quiet and the shadow of the Civil War had not
yet fallen upon the territory.

Later, difficulties with the Indians and the approach of the Civil War were to make the administration of Governor Rencher a stormy one, and provide a poor climate for poetry, of which Rencher wrote:

> Poetry is not merely an ornament which charms us with its sounds. In poetry, we behold the heart, the feelings and the passions exposed to our view, as we behold countries, cities and mountains on the landscape. . . .[7]

Abraham Rencher, tall, high-colored, with piercing brown eyes, was born in North Carolina in 1798. He was graduated from the University of North Carolina Law School in 1822. At thirty-one, he was elected to the twenty-first Congress and served for ten years.

The new governor arrived in Santa Fe with his wife and daughters on November 11, 1857. David Meriwether had departed in May 1857, and on October 15, 1857, acting governor W. W. H. Davis left Santa Fe for the states.[8] This left the territory without a governor and without a territorial secretary, and the offices had been left in charge of Samuel Ellison, private secretary to the acting governor.[9]

Governor Rencher began work immediately. After visiting the leading citizens of the territory, he drafted his first address to the legislature. He delivered the address on December 9, 1857, speaking enthusiastically of the possibilities of New Mexico and giving the first economic development address to a New Mexico legislature:

> Your mines of gold, silver, copper, and lead are said to be not inferior to those of California. . . . It is true we are too remote from commerce to be able to manufacture iron for other states, but surely we should not continue to

buy them [sic] at five times the price for which we could
manufacture a better article at home. . . .

This country is distinguished for its pasturage. Your
flocks and your herds constitute much of your wealth, and
yet your surplus wool must rot on the dunghill, or be sent
across the plains to be manufactured and brought back here
and sold to you, at four or five times the price for which
you could manufacture as good an article at home. . . .

Equally important to the Territory is the improvement of her agriculture. . . . Every improvement, therefore, in agriculture is an individual as well as a national
benefit, which is only a repetition of the maxim, that he
should be considered a public benefactor, who makes two
blades of grass to grow where only one grew before. . . .

If, for example, by the introduction of the Chinese
sugar cane, we could manufacture our own sugar, how important it could be to the people, and what a saving to the
Territory!

As had the earlier governors, Governor Rencher spoke of the
need for public education:

I should do great injustice to this interesting occasion
if I failed to bring to your favorable notice the great cause
of education. Not simply the education of the rich by the
endowment of colleges, but the education of the masses by
common schools. In a government like ours, depending
essentially, as it does upon public opinion, it is all important that public opinion be enlightened. Public schools,
therefore, for the education of those who are not able to
educate themselves, ought to be the first duty of every
statesman and patriot. . . .

Discussing finances, Rencher pointed out that warrants
drawn for the fiscal year ending November 15, 1857, were in

the amount of $10,973, with only $7,664 cash received, making a deficit of $3,309. This, added to the previous debts, totaled $9,872, and he suggested the need of an ad valorem tax to remedy the situation. He was to continue to plead for additional revenue during his four years in New Mexico.

Because of the small remuneration and the great depreciation of territorial warrants by which it was paid, the offices of attorney general and circuit attorney became vacant and government began to break down in 1858.

"If we would have our lives and property protected, we must pay some little to support the government which does exist," the governor said.[10]

During his first year as governor, the trouble with the Navajos began which was to develop into Rencher's greatest problem. The Navajos were attempting to live in peace in 1858, but military commanders and Indian agents were too eager to set all rules for the Indians' behavior. In the spring, the military killed sixty horses belonging to the Navajos because the animals were allowed to graze on grass set aside for the cavalry at Fort Defiance. The Indians did not retaliate.

Then, on July 11, 1858, a Negro boy was shot by a Navajo at Fort Defiance. The boy was the slave of Major W. T. W. Brooks, post commandant. Brooks demanded the surrender of the Navajo on a murder charge. The Navajos were willing to make payment according to their custom, but Major Brooks insisted upon delivery of the guilty Indian within twenty days. In order to enforce his ultimatum and avoid losing prestige, Major Brooks recommended war.[11]

War broke out on September 9, when Lt. Col. D. S. Miles, with three hundred men, took to the field. The war would be waged spasmodically for the duration of Rencher's administration.

Always an independent administrator, Rencher criti-

cized the military in writing to Secretary of State Lewis Cass
on October 16, 1858:

> I did not approve of the manner in which we have
> been precipitated into this war by the independent action
> of the commander of the post at Fort Defiance. It seemed
> to me that Major Brooks should have referred the matter to
> the head of the department before taking such steps as was
> [sic] likely to result in hostilities. . . . The Indian agent
> was present, and instead of protesting against so hasty and
> unauthorized a movement, seems to have approved it. I
> fear . . . there has been at Fort Defiance too ready a dis-
> position to engage in active hostilities with the Navajos. . .
>
> If the war continues, the inevitable result must be that
> their flocks [will be] destroyed, and their cornfields laid
> waste, they will become more dependent upon us for sup-
> port and more reckless in their marauding incursions upon
> our people. . . .[12]

An early poem of Rencher's seemed to describe the situation in these lines:

> A land deluged in blood without a cause,
> Thou monster, look on thy path![13]

A Santa Fe *Gazette* story of October 9, 1858, reported:

> The principal guide of the troops is a Pueblo Indian
> from Zuni. He is a small, erect, well formed Indian, and
> wears his thick raven hair hanging down to the middle of
> his back. In the scout to Cañon de Chelle, one of the pri-
> soners taken was handed over to the Mexicans and the guide
> to be disposed of.
>
> It was agreed that the Zuni should be the executioner.
> The Navajo was soon placed at a short distance off, when

Zuni raised his old flintlock to do his duty. The Navajo appealed, 'Oh don't . . . kill me, my friend!' Zuni very gravely responded, 'Porque, Porque?'—'Why not, why not?' This very rational and reasonable question not being satisfactorily answered to Zuni's notion of the ethics of war, he took deliberate aim, sent a leaden messenger through Mr. Navajo's brain, thus ushering his untutored spirit into the blissful regions of the great hunting ground. Zuni was much delighted with the amusement and says he will be made a big chief when he returns home . . .

Rencher was outraged by the incident and sent the report to Secretary Cass with his comment:

> The letter encloses a piece of brutality worthy only of the most degraded savages. But for the sources from whence it comes and the apparent approval of the Indian agent, I should doubt the truth of the statement. . . . I am sure the conduct of the commanding officer in permitting such savage brutality will be condemned by Colonel B. L. E. Bonneville, the present commander of the department. . . .[14]

The gentleman from North Carolina was taking a firmer position as executive of the territory.

The Navajo war ended with an armistice November 20, 1858. Governor Rencher, in a special legislative message, criticized the war and the armistice, saying:

> If . . . the Indians have been castigated and humbled, as our Indian agent says they have, we ought to be glad of it. . . . The armistice provided only for the surrender by the Indians of property taken from the Fort and which belonged to the United States, but did not provide for the surrender of private property taken by the Indians during the

war from the citizens of the Territory. The armistice did not provide for the surrender of the murderer, which was the cause of the war, nor even for the payment of the negro boy who was murdered. . . .[15]

The Indians remained quiet until April 30, 1859. On that date, they boldly attacked Fort Defiance. They were driven off without serious loss on either side. This is the only instance of New Mexico Indians attacking a strongly garrisoned post, although in the two years, 1859 and 1860, a total of nearly three hundred citizens were killed by them.[16]

Governor Rencher wrote to Secretary Cass on February 4, 1860:

> The Indian depredation in this territory has become so frequent and so aggravated that public excitement is very great. The main mail route to the states has been in the hands of the Kiowas for the last six months. The Navajos are adding to the list of old wrongs other depredations and murders almost every day. This has resulted in an angry session of the legislature.[17]

The governor incurred the enmity of the legislature, the citizens, and the military commanders in his attempts to handle the Indians. Later, the citizens were to ask for his removal as governor.

The Indians grew bolder. In July, several citizens were murdered by Indians ten miles from Santa Fe. The Santa Fe *Gazette* of August 22, 1860, reported that forty-four men pursued a group of Navajo Indians who killed several men and injured others within the limits of the county of Santa Fe. They overtook the Indians at eleven o'clock in the morning and fought until five in the afternoon when the Indians retreated. The pursuers reported that there were sixty Indians. Of the pursuers, three were killed and five wounded, three seriously. Thirteen Indians were killed and several wounded in the action.

The same issue of the *Gazette* offered this comment:

> . . . your spiritual fathers are exhausted in their sad labor of ministering the mournful rites of sepulture to your dead, and of tendering the consolations of our holy faith to their surviving and sorrowing friends . . . the government which had pledged you its protection, has apparently abandoned you to your fate; and though your despairing cries arose to heaven, they involved no earthly aid. . . .

The people of the territory held a convention in Santa Fe, August 29, 1860, to determine if they should take the Navajo War into their own hands. They voted to raise volunteers under citizen leadership for a Navajo campaign. Governor Rencher was in sympathy with the citizens, but he noted that the governor had no ammunition and no power to raise any.

The new military commander of troops stationed in the territory, Col. Thomas T. Fauntleroy, declared on October 15, 1859, that, if the governor authorized a campaign under the law, he would withdraw the regular troops from the Indian country.

After the citizen's convention, Rencher wrote to Secretary Cass for instructions. Lewis Cass replied, November 24, 1860: "The Department sees no justification for the unauthorized organization of a volunteer force to make war upon the Navajo Indians."[18] Cass' reply forced Rencher to take a position opposing the volunteers.

In October, Governor Rencher wrote to Secretary Cass:

> The volunteer forces raised in August of which I in-
> formed you have gone, without authority of law, into the
> Navajo country, leaving their homes unprotected . . .
>
> Our Indian trouble continues without abatement; in-
> deed the Navajos are more daring in their robberies than
> at any previous time. They seized and carried off at two
> o'clock in the day upwards of two hundred mules from
> within eight miles of the city.[19]

The volunteers returned in January without having accomplished much. They wanted Congress to pay them for
their unauthorized fighting. A measure authorizing $50,000
in territorial bonds to be issued to the volunteers was introduced and passed in the legislature. In withholding his approval of the measure, Rencher wrote:

> I have repeatedly stated in the most public form that
> the military expedition, for which this bill proposes to bur-
> den the Territory with a heavy and ruinous debt was un-
> necessary, unauthorized by law, and unsuccessful in its re-
> sults. I could not, therefore, approve any measure of this
> kind without a violation of my oath of office.
>
> The act authorizing the $50,000 in bonds provided
> no means for paying them. Their object was, under the ad-
> vice of the delegate in Congress, to make the claim more
> plausible before Congress. . . . My position has imposed
> upon me an unpleasant duty which has brought upon me
> the displeasure of the Legislative Assembly. They have
> even asked my removal for my opposition to this unjust
> imposition upon the Federal Government. . . .[20]

The volunteer campaign and the campaign of the regu-

lar army were both indecisive. An armistice was negotiated.
The formal cessation of hostilities continued all during 1861
because of the uncertainties arising from the outbreak of the
Civil War.

During the Indian troubles of 1859-60, Governor Rencher and Col. Thomas T. Fauntleroy, the military commander, had sharp differences which led, eventually, to a break.
Rencher, the romanticist and dreamer, had little time in
New Mexico to philosophize and write poetry as before, but
he employed some of his best prose on the subject of Colonel
Fauntleroy:

> The land sharks, who surround Colonel Fauntleroy
> and instill seductive flattery into his too willing ears, wish
> to make a magnificent expedition at the expense of a thou-
> sand volunteers, that there may be thrown into the market
> a thousand land claims and other claims for them to feed
> on. . . .[21]

Fauntleroy wrote to Rencher:

> . . . I have just received a copy of a letter you wrote
> to the Secretary of State of the United States, 4 February,
> 1860. As this letter seems to insinuate that I have been
> actuated in my course in the command of this department
> by improper motives and with the view of aiding specula-
> tors in procuring land claims, I request that you will,
> without any doubts as to the purpose and meaning of your
> letter, say whether you in any manner whatever mean to
> impute to me conduct that could reflect upon my charac-
> ter.[22]

There was further trouble when the governor prepared
to use materials from an old post office to repair the Palace.

Of this matter, Rencher wrote to Secretary Cass:

> . . . the post office . . . has been vacated for some
> time as untenable. Very much to my surprise, if I could be
> surprised by anything from that quarter, Colonel Fount-
> leroy caused to be sent to me an order forbidding me to
> employ the material of the old post office, and even threat-
> ened me with martial law if I continued to take it down.[23]

The trouble between Colonel Fauntleroy and Governor Rencher was never resolved, for the Colonel resigned
from the Union army and fought on the side of the Confederacy.

In spite of the Indian wars, Governor Rencher achieved
two important legislative objectives.

On January 27, 1860, a measure was passed providing
that all persons of school age must attend school. (The number of illiterates in 1860 was 57,233 of a non-Indian population of 82,979.) Under the education act, teachers received
fifty cents from each child per month. The local justices of
the peace were responsible for the schools, appointing the
teachers, inspecting schools, and removing teachers in cases
of incompetency.[24]

Rencher was also successful in helping the territory improve its financial position. In 1857, the total debt of the territory was $9,872. In his final legislative message, December
6, 1860, Rencher reported that for the preceding twelve
months there was a surplus of $762, reducing the total debt
to $3,673. He added: "The auditor states that some of the
counties have not made full returns, that if they had done so,
I should have been able to announce to the legislature the
gratifying fact that the Territory was out of debt. . . ."[25]

During the last two years of his administration, slavery

was the most urgent public question. As early as 1848, New Mexico had expressed a firm desire to remain free of slavery. A citizens' convention, authorized by the legislature, met October 10, 1848, and memorialized Congress:

> We do not desire to have domestic slavery within our borders; until the time shall arrive for admission into the Union of States, we desire to be protected by Congress against the introduction of slaves into the territory.[26]

The Constitutional Convention in Santa Fe in 1850 resolved:

> Slavery in New Mexico is naturally impracticable and can never, in reality, exist here . . . we have unanimously agreed to reject it forever. . . .[27]

However, from the beginning of territorial government in 1851, the official attitude toward slavery began to change. The majority of appointments to New Mexico were men of the South. James S. Calhoun, of Georgia, first territorial governor, mentioned free Negroes to the first territorial legislature:

> Free Negroes are regarded as nuisances in every state and territory in the Union, and where they are tolerated Society is most depraved. I trust the legislature will pass a law that will prevent their entrance into this Territory.[28]

The legislature waited until 1856 to pass an act restricting the activities of free Negroes. By its provisions, no free Negro could remain in New Mexico for more than thirty days.

The adoption of this measure reflected the growing influence of Southerners in territorial politics. Then, during

Rencher's administration, Southern control was tightened by the alignment of Miguel Otero (territorial congressional delegate, 1855-61) with Southern political leaders and institutions. New Mexico so completely reversed its earlier sentiments toward slavery that it adopted a slave code in 1859.[29]

Alexander M. Jackson, formerly of Mississippi, wrote on August 16, 1858:

> It is generally believed that the territorial legislature will pass some kind of slave code for the territory at the next session. . . . Otero has let it be known that if New Mexico expects any favors from Washington, a slave code would be a wise move. The Governor [Rencher] and most of the other officials are favorable to it. . . .[30]

Both legislative houses passed the slave code, and it was signed by Governor Rencher February 3, 1859. This measure was for the protection of slave property and to define the status of slaves. The adoption of a slave code was accepted generally as New Mexico's final alignment with Southern principles. In 1860, it appeared that New Mexico would follow the leadership of the Southern states. Rencher commented on the slave code: "The legislature can neither create nor abolish slavery. They can only regulate it where it already exists, as any other species of property. . . ."[31]

By 1861, New Mexico civil and military leaders were choosing their allegiances. New Mexico's military leaders, Thomas T. Fauntleroy, Henry H. Sibley and William W. Loring, resigned to join the Confederate Army. But Rencher, a transplanted North Carolina Democrat, remained loyal to the Union.

A citizens' convention was held in March at Mesilla in southern New Mexico, declaring in favor of the Confederacy. At this point, a St. Louis newspaper accused the governor of leading a Confederate revolution and capturing Fort Marcy in Santa Fe. Rumors questioning his loyalty circulated in Santa Fe and Washington. But Rencher, true to his ideals and his oath, wrote to President Lincoln's Secretary of State, William H. Seward, on April 20, 1861:

> The people of Santa Fe are a law abiding people and loyal to the Union; the governor, I well know, never expressed or entertained any other sentiment. . . .
>
> [I regret] existing national difficulties and . . . have an . . . anxious desire that they might ultimately be compromised upon some permanent and peaceful basis. . . .
>
> In all the popular meetings which I have noticed, the people express great attachment to the Union, and an earnest desire that it may be preserved. . . .[32]

The attitude of many New Mexicans was expressed in an editorial, appearing in the Santa Fe *Gazette,* May 11, 1861:

> What is the position of New Mexico? The answer is a short one. She desires to be let alone. No interferences from one side or the other of the sections that are now waging war. She neither wants abolitionists nor secessionists from abroad to mix in her affairs at present; nor will she tolerate either. In her own good time, she will say her say, and choose for herself the position she wishes to occupy in the new disposition of the now disrupted power of the United States.

Abraham Rencher, the philosopher who felt at home in the capitals of Europe, felt as much at home in the Gov-

ernor's Palace in Santa Fe. After four years there, he indicated that he would accept another term if it were offered to
him by President Lincoln. In offering his resignation to Secretary Seward, he did not close the door upon a new appointment:

> My term of office will expire next winter. If it shall be
> the pleasure of the president before that period to appoint
> some more suitable person to discharge the duties of my
> place, I beg that I may be notified of it in time to enable me
> to arrange in advance for my departure.[33]

The notification that he was not to be reappointed came in
the spring of 1861.

When Fort Fillmore, below Las Cruces, fell to Texas
troops July 26, 1861, Governor Rencher issued a proclamation that held New Mexico firmly in the Union:

> I, Abraham Rencher, Governor of the Territory of
> New Mexico, by virtue of my authority as Governor of said
> Territory, do call upon all good and loyal citizens to uphold
> the authority of the laws and to defend the Territory
> against invasion and violence from whatever quarter they
> may come. For this purpose, I exhort and require all per-
> sons able to do military service to organize themselves into
> military companies.[34]

The same week, he wrote to Secretary Seward:

> Recently that portion of the Territory . . . known
> as Arizona has been invaded by troops from Texas, and all
> the military posts in that part of the Territory have been
> taken or abandoned. All the facts connected with this un-
> fortunate affair have doubtless been laid before the Secre-
> tary of War.[35]

May 22, 1860, the Santa Fe Weekly *Gazette* expressed the opinion of many New Mexicans, in writing of Governor Rencher: "He has our interests as much at heart as if he had been chosen by the free suffrages of the people."

Late in August 1861, when Rencher turned the office of governor over to his successor, New Mexico was safe for the Union—thanks, in part, to a true patriot from North Carolina.

NOTES

1. *The National Cyclopaedia of American Biography, being the History of the United States,* New York, White & Co., 1898.

2. *Abraham Rencher Papers,* Chapel Hill, University of North Carolina Library.

3. *Territorial Papers of the U.S. Department of State, New Mexico,* March 3, 1851—Dec. 8, 1860, National Archives, Washington.

4. *Ibid.*

5. *Ibid.*

6. *Abraham Rencher Papers, op. cit.*

7. *Ibid.*

8. A. B. Bender, "Frontier Defense in the Territory of New Mexico," *The New Mexico Historical Review,* v. IX, October 1934.

9. *Territorial Papers of the U. S. Department of State, op. cit.*

10. *Ibid.*

11. Frank D. Reeve, "The Federal Indian Policy in New Mexico," *The New Mexico Historical Review,* v. XII, July 1937.

12. *Territorial Papers of the U.S. Department of State, op. cit.*

13. *Abraham Rencher Papers, op. cit.*

14. *Territorial Papers of the U.S. Department of State, op. cit.*

15. *Ibid.*

16. Ralph E. Twitchell, *The Leading Facts of New Mexican History,* v. II, Cedar Rapids, Torch, 1912.

17. *Territorial Papers of the U.S. Department of State, op. cit.*

18. *Ibid.*

19. *Ibid.*

20. *Territorial Papers of the U.S. Department of State, op. cit.,* Jan. 2, 1861—Dec. 23, 1864.

21. *Territorial Papers of the U.S. Department of State, op. cit.,* March 3, 1851—Dec. 8, 1860.

22. *Ibid.*

23. *Ibid.*

24. Charles F. Coan, *A History of New Mexico,* Chicago, The American Historical Society, 1925.

25. *Territorial Papers of the U.S. Department of State, op. cit.* March 3, 1851—Dec. 8, 1860.

26. Ralph E. Twitchell, *The History of the Military Occupation of the Territory of New Mexico, from 1846 to 1851 by the Govt. of the United States,* Denver, Smith-Brooks, 1909.

27. Loomis Morton Gannaway, *New Mexico and the Sectional Controversy, 1846-1861,* Albuquerque, Univ. of New Mexico, 1944.

28. *Territorial Papers of the U. S. Department of State, op.* cit., March 3, 1851—Dec. 8, 1860.

29. Ralph E. Twitchell, *Old Santa Fe: the Story of New Mexico's Ancient Capital* (ed. and written with trans. by R. E. Twitchell), Santa Fe, New Mexico Publishing Corp., 1925.

30. *Territorial Papers of the U.S. Department of State, op. cit.,* March 3, 1851—Dec. 8, 1860.

31. *Ibid.*

32. *Territorial Papers of the U.S. Department of State, op. cit.,* Jan. 2, 1861—Dec. 23, 1864.

33. *Ibid.*

34. *Ibid.*

35. *Ibid.*

HENRY CONNELLY

FIVE

Civil War Governor

HENRY CONNELLY

1861-66

PRESIDENT ABRAHAM LINCOLN SELECTED NEW MEXICO'S widely known and respected leader, Dr. Henry Connelly, to succeed Abraham Rencher as governor of New Mexico. Doctor Connelly, who received a medical degree in Lexington, Kentucky, had lived in New Mexico for nearly forty years and had already served his adopted home in several capacities.

His letter of acceptance, dated June 29, 1861, was short and modest:

> I have the honor to inform you that I will accept the high position which the President has been pleased to confer upon me.
>
> I was born in the state of Virginia [1800], but at the age of four years, my father immigrated to Kentucky, where I lived until 1824. Since then, I have been, most of the time, a resident of this Territory.[1]

Connelly had put down roots in the territory. He knew Mexican leaders from long residence in Mexico. He owned his first store in Chihuahua, Mexico, in 1830. In 1838 he married a Mexican woman; they had three boys, but she soon died. One of the boys, Peter eventually became clerk of the New Mexico territorial supreme court.[2]

In 1839, Henry Connelly attempted to find a new route from Chihuahua across Texas directly to Independence, Missouri, for the benefit of Mexican merchants. In that year, he led a caravan of one hundred men who made the trip through Texas to Missouri and returned to Chihuahua a year later, but the journey was never repeated.[3]

Connelly formed a partnership in 1842 with Edward J. Glasgow to engage in trade between Independence and Chihuahua. Glasgow wrote of Connelly:

> Dr. Connelly had already been in business several years in Chihuahua, was moderately well off and in good standing and credit as a merchant of ability, integrity, and fair dealing, besides enjoying the personal friendship of many of the influential Mexicans and all of his own countrymen in that city. . . .[4]

By the time of his appointment to the office of governor, Connelly had married a second time—the widow of Don Mariano Chavez and daughter of Don Pedro Perea—and he and his wife lived in a lovely home at Peralta near one of his large mercantile stores.[5]

Even before the United States occupation of New Mexico, Henry Connelly had served in an important role. As a close friend of Manuel Armijo, governor of the Mexican state of New Mexico, Connelly entered into negotiations between Mexican and U.S. leaders at a crucial time.

In the summer of 1846, Gen. Stephen Watts Kearny, with 1,658 men, was marching toward New Mexico, planning to take the area for the United States. Before marching into New Mexico from Bent's Fort in Colorado, General Kearny sent James Magoffin and Capt. Philip St. George

Cook ahead of the army to confer with Governor Armijo. James Magoffin was an excellent choice for emissary. He was a well-known New Mexico trader whose wife was related to Armijo. Magoffin was also a friend of Senator Thomas Hart Benton and of President James Polk.

On August 12, 1846, Magoffin and Cook arrived in Santa Fe. The city was alive with preparations for war. Some 3,000 armed volunteers crowded the village. Earlier in the week, Governor Armijo had issued a war proclamation, asserting that he was "ready to sacrifice his life and interest for his beloved country." A defense meeting was held in Santa Fe, attended by the most influential citizens with Col. Diego Archuleta, able soldier and capable politician, in charge. When envoys Magoffin and Cook arrived, they were protected from the plaza mob by an escort of twelve soldiers.

In his diary, Captain Cook described his arrival at the Palace of the Governors: "I entered from the hall, a large and lofty apartment with a carpeted earth floor, and discovered the Governor seated at a table with six or eight military and civil officials standing."[6] One of the officials standing was Henry Connelly.

The evening of August 12, Governor Armijo, accompanied by his friend Connelly, held a dinner conference with Magoffin and Cook. Captain Cook wrote in his diary: "At 10 P.M. General Armijo came. . . . It was settled that a 'commissioner' should return with me and that we should set out at sunrise. . . . I was accompanied on my return by the 'commissioner', Dr. Connelly, an Englishman."[7] (Actually, Connelly was of Irish descent, but American born.)

Connelly met General Kearny at Tecolote, near Las Vegas, for a conference. No record exists of their conversations. But, three days later, on August 16, Governor Armijo rode to Apache Canyon where his troops stood ready to defend New Mexico and ordered the soldiers to return to their homes. Within a few hours, the troops had dispersed.[8]

Armijo's reasons for giving the order which permitted the bloodless conquest of New Mexico are not absolutely clear. Somehow, the August 12 meeting had produced success for the United States, and Henry Connelly was the principal intermediary between his friend Armijo and General Kearny. One soldier's diary suggested a possible reason for Armijo's withdrawal:

> Connelly's report as to the number and condition of the American army created a panic among the officials, and was the principal cause of the abandonment of New Mexico by Armijo.[9]

James Magoffin also appears to have been influential in bringing about the change of attitudes on the part of Armijo and Archuleta. Sometime later, when Magoffin was reimbursed by the War Department for his expenses during the war, he was given $2,000 "for entertainment to officers, military and civil, and to influential citizens of Santa Fe, Chihuahua, and Durango, to accomplish the object of promoting the interests of the United States."[10]

On August 18, 1846, General Kearny rode into Santa Fe and occupied New Mexico without firing a shot. Henry Connelly had been of real service to the United States.

Immediately after the occupation, Governor Armijo fled to Chihuahua, Mexico. Connelly wrote to General Armijo asking him to return:

> . . . I at once saw General Kearny. He has assured me that your person and interests are as secure as if General Armijo governed. . . . You will surrender the authority of Governor and commandant with the forces which accompany it. . . .

I advise you, my dear friend, to return to Santa Fe without delay . . . Until you should be pleased to present yourself to General Kearny do not fear, General Armijo. For all the above I answer with my life, as the friend which I am.[11]

Because he was interested in resuming trade with Mexico, Connelly rode to El Paso early in November 1846, in advance of the army, to ascertain upon what conditions merchandise could be sent into Chihuahua. He was arrested in El Paso by Mexican officers; his papers were taken; he was escorted by twenty-six soldiers to Chihuahua, and placed in jail. James Magoffin's sister, Susan, wrote on December 1:

News comes in very ugly today. . . . the three traders, Dr. Conley [sic], Frank McManus, and brother James, who went on ahead to Chihuahua, have been taken prisoners, the two former lodged in the calabozo, while Brother James is on trial for his life, on account of his interview with Armijo at Santa Fe, which they say was one cause of the latter's having acted as he did in regard to the American army. . . .[12]

Henry Connelly was soon released and Magoffin's life was saved, possibly by the intervention of Armijo.

After the Mexicans were defeated at the Battle of Sacramento, fifteen miles north of Chihuahua, the U.S. Commander, Col. Alexander William Doniphan, sent Henry Connelly to Parral, Mexico, to discuss conditions of peace with Governor Angel Trias and to invite Trias to return to Chihuahua. The governor refused to return.

In 1850, the people of New Mexico demonstrated that they valued Connelly's services in the Mexican War, holding him in high regard. That year, anticipating statehood, a constitutional convention was held. When the constitution was submitted to the people for ratification, Henry Connelly's name was offered as a candidate for governor. The constitution was adopted and Connelly was elected by a large majority. However, Congress failed to grant statehood and Connelly, therefore, did not serve.

When New Mexico gained recognition as a territory in 1851, Doctor Connelly was soon elected to the Territorial Council—as the State Senate was then called. He served in the Council from Bernalillo County from 1853 until 1859.

When Governor Manuel Armijo died on December 9, 1853, at his home near Lemitar, New Mexico, Henry Connelly, loyal to his old friend, offered a resolution in the Council which was unanimously adopted:

> Resolved, that this Council has heard with profound regret the death of our distinguished citizen, Gen. Armijo . . . the Council offers the most sincere condolence to the family and friends of Gen. Armijo and to the territory for the loss of one of its greatest benefactors. . . .[13]

Governor Henry Connelly, the first territorial governor to be appointed from the territory, was sworn in September 4, 1861.

Union forces were on the defensive the day Connelly became governor. The Confederate flag flew over many places in New Mexico. During the preceding summer, Texans had occupied Fort Bliss, had taken Fort Fillmore near Mesilla, and had captured seven hundred Union troops. Gen. Henry Hopkins Sibley was equipping and training a Confederate force of 3,500 men at San Antonio with the object of capturing New Mexico.

With Connelly as governor and Col. Edward R. S. Canby as military commander, New Mexico was now in the hands of strong Union administrators. Five days after his inauguration, September 9, Governor Connelly issued a proclamation:

> Whereas, this Territory is now invaded by armed force from the State of Texas, which has taken possession of two Forts within the limits of the Territory, has seized and appropriated to its own use other property of the Territorial Government, and has established military rule over the part already invaded . . . I, Henry Connelly . . . do hereby issue this my Proclamation, ordering an immediate organization of the Militia force in the different counties of this Territory, and calling upon all Officers, Civil and Military, to begin at once this organization. . . .
>
> Citizens of New Mexico, your Territory has been invaded, the integrity of your soil has been attacked, the property of peaceful and industrious citizens has been destroyed or converted to the use of the invaders, and the enemy is already at your doors. You cannot, you must not, hesitate to take up arms in defense of your homes, firesides and families. . . .[14]

In Governor Connelly's first legislative message, December 4, 1861, he said:

> No people on the face of the earth were as free, as happy, and as prosperous as were those of the United States before the heresy of secessionism burst out into open rebellion . . .
>
> [I plead for] the maintenance of the holy cause, which I must devoutly pray may be crowned with success, and that the Ruler of the Universe will, in the plenitude of His wisdom and power, restore our distracted country to its former prosperous and happy condition . . .
>
> The enemy is Texas and the Texans. [They threaten] under the pretence that they are under the authority of a

new arrangement they call a Confederacy, but in truth is
a rebel organization. . . .

Be true, be faithful, and be courageous; then . . .
New Mexico will blaze with fame, and her sons and daughters glow with pride. . . . Now is the day to feel the ting-
lings of the ancient and unconquerable Castillian blood
that our ancestors brought to this land. . . .[15]

Connelly demanded the repeal of the Slave Act of 1859
which protected slavery in the territory. After the repeal of
the act, on December 10, 1861, he declared: "We have condemned, and put slavery from among our laws. It is not con-
genial with our history. . . ."[16]

Southern leaders recognized that the stakes in New Mexico were high—mineral wealth, munitions stored in the territory, prestige to be gained in Europe by a victory, a gate-
way to California. The Texans, remembering the ill-fated invasion of New Mexico in 1841, were ready to fight. Confederate strategists assumed that there was much dissatisfaction
among New Mexico soldiers and that the territory would
easily fall.[17]

The last part of January 1862, Governor Connelly left
Santa Fe for Fort Craig, where the first major battle was
expected. Fort Craig was located on the Rio Grande above
the village that is now Truth or Consequences. He wrote to
Secretary of State W. H. Seward, January 23, 1862: "I leave
tomorrow for the seat of war, not only from a sense of duty,
but by a special request from the Colonel Commanding."[18]
The governor recruited volunteer soldiers as he made his
way south.

From Fort Craig, Connelly reported to Seward that the
Union had 4,000 men under arms, while the enemy exceeded
3,000. "We have now no fear of any serious reverse to our
arms," he concluded.[19]

The forces of the Union and the Confederacy met in February near Fort Craig in what came to be called the Battle of Valverde—said to be perhaps the bloodiest battle for the number engaged in the whole war.

From a vantage point, Governor Connelly watched the formation of the battle lines between Gen. Henry H. Sibley's Confederate forces and the Union regiments commanded by Col. Edward R. S. Canby. The fighting had been delayed several days by dust storms, but finally began on February 21, 1862.

Connelly saw the Confederate forces attempt a crossing of the river then fall back under a Union counter-charge. Then, as the Union troops began to cross the river, the Confederates opened a terrific fire and charged the Union batteries with everything, including shotguns.

"Never were double barreled shotguns used to better effect,"[20] a witness said. A unit of the Union forces reached the east side of the river but the troops were overrun. Within six hours after the charge, the Confederates had won. Canby ordered a retreat to the fort.

With heavy heart, Connelly witnessed the defeat. When he was sure the Confederate troops were victorious, he rode to Peralta, where he had his home and store. He distributed his cattle, merchandise and equipment to the people of Peralta to prevent seizure by Confederate forces.[21]

Upon returning to Santa Fe, the governor wrote to Secretary of State Seward, describing the battle of Valverde and the progress of the Texans who were moving toward Santa Fe and Fort Union. By March 2, they had raised the Confederate flag in Albuquerque. He wrote: "I am sorry to say that the Texans have not behaved with the moderation that was expected, and that desolation has marked their progress on the Rio Grande from Craig to Bernalillo. . . ."[22]

Governor Connelly and the troops abandoned Santa Fe on March 4, moving to Las Vegas and Fort Union with 120 wagons of supplies. Connelly wrote to Secretary Seward on March 11:

> The Capitol, having been abandoned by the U.S. forces, I came in company with them, and I have for the present established the Executive Department at Las Vegas, 30 miles West of this post. . . . Should the forces at this place unite with Col. Canby, the enemy will be driven from the Territory. Should Col. Canby be attacked by the enemy and suffer a defeat, we will then be in a very precarious condition until reinforcements arrive. . . . I hope by the next mail to give you the information that the enemy are either vanquished in battle or are in retreat from the Territory.[23]

Santa Fe fell to the Confederate forces on March 23. The Confederates established a territorial government at Santa Fe and announced that citizens would be required to swear Confederate allegiance or suffer loss of their property. On March 25, Confederate troops marched toward Fort Union and the decisive battle of the Civil War in New Mexico.

The battle began on March 26, at Glorieta, located between Santa Fe and Las Vegas. Both sides fired their cannons and immediately retreated.

Early on March 28, Col. John M. Chivington of the Union troops circled to the rear of the Texans, found their supply trains and attacked. Connelly reported to Seward, March 30, 1862:

> Major Chivington with 500 men had been ordered to make a detour on the heights . . . he found the enemy's whole train packed together . . . guarded by 200 men.

He made a sudden and unexpected attack upon them, and captured the whole train of 80 wagons. . . .

Connelly said that Chivington burned the wagons, bayonetted the mules and destroyed all the Texans' supplies. He added that the Union losses for the two-day encounter, killed, wounded and missing, would total 150, and estimated the losses of the enemy at 300.[24]

At the time of Major Chivington's attack, rumors were passed among the Confederate troops that Colonel Canby was attacking in the rear. Actually, Canby was 140 miles to the south, at Socorro.

After the battle at Glorieta, both armies again retreated. The Union troops went to Fort Union. The Texans, thinking themselves badly whipped, retired from the area. The Confederate commander reported:

> The loss of my supplies so crippled me that after burying my dead I was unable to follow up the victory. My men for two days went unfed and blanketless. . . . I was compelled to come to Santa Fe for something to eat.[25]

Union forces, although they did not immediately realize it, had dealt a death blow to the hopes of the Confederacy. Connelly was disappointed that the Union troops had withdrawn: "So it turned out that had our troops advanced the day after the battle, it would have led to the entire capture and dispersal of the enemy's force in the neighborhood of Santa Fe. . . ."[26]

Several minor skirmishes occurred between Union and Texas forces before the Texans retreated to El Paso. The Battle of Albuquerque was fought April 10, when each side fired their cannons. Canby stopped firing when the townspeople complained.

The last skirmish took place April 18, 1862, near Peralta. The Texans had taken over Governor Connelly's home there. When Canby (now a general) arrived late at night he heard sounds of revelry. The enemy seemed to be entirely unconscious of his approach.

Of the occupation of his home by Confederate forces, Connelly wrote: "My loss has been very heavy."[27] And in another letter: "There was much about the house of goods and furniture that they could put to no useful purpose, yet all was taken or wantonly destroyed."[28] Connelly estimated his losses at $30,000.

At the Battle of Peralta the Union forces were successful in forcing the Confederates to cross the Rio Grande to the west bank, abandoning their supply trains except rations sufficient for seven days. It was reported that "Their teams being weak and the river swollen by the Spring flood, the whole of their train, consisting of 60 wagons, was left in the river and on the banks. . . ."[29]

The Confederate troops retreated through the mountains in order to pass Fort Craig without further conflict, and this was the end of the Texan invasion. It was estimated by a subordinate of Canby that only 1,200 of the 3,000 Texans were able to leave the territory.

Governor Connelly left Las Vegas April 14, returning the seat of government to Santa Fe. Under his leadership, New Mexico was still safely in the Union and rid of the invading Texans.

The governor now turned his attention to the age-old New Mexico problem—the Indians. As a long-time New Mexico resident, Governor Henry Connelly knew the Indians. He applied himself to solving the problem permanently. He was joined in his resolution by the new military commander, Gen. James H. Carleton, who succeeded Canby. Their plan was to kill the Indians, regardless of rules of war or mercy,

or place them upon reservations. Connelly made his attitude
clear:

> [The power of the government] should be so directed
> as to keep these sons of the forest within proper limits and
> either maintain them as paupers, teach them the arts of
> civilized life and oblige them to sustain themselves, or, on
> the other hand, exterminate them.[30]

General Carleton expressed a similar point of view:

> It may be set down as a rule that the Navajo Indians
> have long since passed that point when talking would be
> of any avail. They must be whipped and fear us before they
> will cease killing and robbing the people.[31]

The two leaders decided upon a reservation, an area
forty miles square near Fort Sumner, called the Bosque Redondo. All troublesome Indians were either to be killed or
located at Bosque Redondo. The plan was to kill or starve
them into absolute submission.

One set of General Carleton's orders to his men read:

> All Indian men of the Mescalero tribe are to be killed
> whenever and wherever you can find them. . . . If the In-
> dians send in a flag and desire to treat for peace, say to the
> bearer that . . . you have no power to make peace; that
> you are there to kill them wherever you find them. . . .
> The Indians are to be soundly whipped, without parleys
> or councils, except as I have told you.[32]

The campaign to subdue the Navajos began in earnest
in 1863 under the leadership of Kit Carson. He set out upon
a systematic campaign to starve them. Navajo wheat and
corn fields were burned; their peach and other fruit trees
were chopped down.

Peaceful Indians were given until July 20, 1863, to surrender voluntarily and go to their new homes on the reservation. On August 23, Governor Connelly wrote to President Lincoln for additional troops:

> To come to the point direct, Mr. President, we need an additional force of at least one mounted regiment in this military department. [If the request is granted] we will never again molest you with the complaint of Indian depredations in New Mexico.[33]

By December 1863, some 1,000 Navajos were traveling to nearby Fort Canby to surrender. Already 500 Navajos waited at the fort, ready for the long trip. The starvation campaign was proving effective. By March, more than 2,000 had been settled at Bosque Redondo. Navajos were taken to the reservation during the following three years. In addition to Navajos, the Gila Apache and the Mescalero Apache tribes were cowed and confined at Bosque Redondo. In January 1865, the reservation population there was 8,557.

General Carleton wrote his plans to the Adjutant General of the Army, September 6, 1863:

> The purpose I have in view is to send all captured Navajos and Apaches to that point [Fort Sumner] and there to feed and take care of them until they have opened farms and become able to support themselves, as the Pueblo Indians of New Mexico are doing.[34]

By 1864, criticism of the reservation plan was growing. The criticism was aimed at Carleton, but soon came to include Governor Connelly. The feeling was that the program of violence against the Indians had no precedent in New Mexico history. Some citizens claimed the Indians were settled upon the best grazing lands—lands too good for the Indians. Others believed that Arizona Indians were being dumped on New Mexico.

Connelly spoke about the criticism: "It is a matter deeply to be regretted that a question should have risen, with any part of our people, as to the propriety of the present locality as an Indian Reservation." [35]

Connelly continued to defend the reservation plan, but his popularity was not sufficient to stop the attacks. The Santa Fe *New Mexican* of October 31, 1864, criticized Carleton for racial, religious and political prejudice.

The year 1865 was the most disastrous for agriculture within the memory of anyone living in the territory. In the Santa Fe *Gazette* on June 17, a reporter wrote: "Properly to describe the misery created by frost, flood, and other combinations of earth and sky this year, a man ought to write with tears instead of ink." The crop failure at the reservation was total. Mescalero and Gila Apaches had been almost exterminated, and thousands of Navajos had been compelled to submit to captivity. There was hunger and misery at Bosque Redondo and thousands of the captives died.

The general disaffection with Carleton was expressed in November 1865, when the Santa Fe *New Mexican* demanded his removal. The following January, the legislature presented a memorial to the Secretary of War condemning Carleton and demanding a court of inquiry as to his stewardship. In September, he was removed.

General Carleton had kept part of New Mexico under martial law since the middle of 1861. In a letter to Carleton January 15, 1864, J. G. Knapp, associate justice of the New Mexico Supreme Court, asked for an end to martial law:

. . . having seen a man shot down in the street by your soldiers; seen the people deprived of their property with-

out compensation or due process of law; having myself twice
suffered incarceration in the guard house. . . .[36]

Governor Connelly had long defended and supported
Carleton. In September 1863, Connelly had written to Secretary of State Seward:

> I have known Gen. Carleton many years ago in this
> territory. He has always been distinguished for his energy,
> zeal and ability. This, together with his exemplary conduct
> in public and private life, has made him a great favorite
> with our people.

In the same letter, Connelly recommended Carleton be pro-
moted to major general and asked Seward to speak to the
President about the promotion.[37]

Connelly's close relationship with Carleton was questioned by Santa Fe legislator Theodore S. Greiner in a letter
to Seward in 1865:

> Foremost in the matter, the friends of Mr. Lincoln have
> found the General commanding that Department, James
> H. Carleton, a 'regular' copperhead, to be their enemy, a
> powerful and unscrupulous enemy. . . . It is fair to the
> amiable incumbent, Governor Connelly, to say that he has
> not been very much of an enemy of Mr. Lincoln as he has
> been a passive tool of the powerful and unscrupulous
> enemy of all Mr. Lincoln's friends in General James H.
> Carleton.
>
> For three years has it been our shame to see daily, often
> hourly, issuing from the Govt. House (the Palacio) the
> family of Governor Connelly wending their way on the
> Plaza to divine service escorted by three or four Navajo
> slaves that have been stolen in raids upon defenseless In-
> dian villages and bought and sold and held as property. . . .[38]

In addition to the outside criticism, Connelly had trouble within his official family. President Lincoln appointed W. F. M. Arny to be secretary of the territory. At first, Arny was trusted by Connelly, who left him in charge of the territory when he had to return to the states for surgery. On another occasion, Connelly sent Arny to Washington with a letter for President Lincoln. Yet Secretary Arny fought Connelly in election matters, attempted to discredit the governor to Secretary Seward, and even returned to Washington at a time when Connelly had specifically ordered him to remain in Santa Fe.

Although he might be dealing with a recalcitrant secretary, fighting the Civil War, or attempting to annihilate an Indian tribe, Governor Connelly constantly worked to improve internal conditions in New Mexico. He believed strongly in education. He wrote:

> Education refines, strengthens and elevates the intellect of man. It purifies society and relieves it from crimes and offenses of every grade and character. It qualifies a people to take the foremost rank in all that goes to make up national and individual greatness. Ignorance and crime, though not inseparable, are, nevertheless, closely linked. . . .[39]

Of the need for industry in the territory, he said:

> The time should not be far distant when the citizens of New Mexico would wear garments made from cloth manufactured in New Mexico, shoes from leather manufactured in New Mexico, walk on floors carpeted with carpets manufactured there; cover their heads with hats of New Mexico; cook their food upon stoves made from New Mexico iron; and ride upon horses shod from iron of native production.

There is no good reason why this should not be experienced within the next four years. . . .[40]

In December 1865, Governor Connelly, in his final message to the legislature, summed up his accomplishments by saying:

I am happy to announce that the present Legislature has assembled under auspices far more favorable to our territory and to our common country than any with which it has been my duty to communicate, during my incumbency in office. . . .[41]

In the Santa Fe *New Mexican* of March 26, 1864, Governor Connelly had been described:

Gov. Connelly is constantly at his post, and ever zealous in the discharge of his trust; all know the amiability and geniality of his temper, disposition and manners. With all this, when the time comes for determination and inflexibility, as the phrase is, 'he is there'. He is no meddler, does not attempt to usurp nor embarrass the official function and duties of others. . . . He harmonizes and sympathizes with all capable and faithful public officers and men of whatever department. . . .

Connelly's official term expired July 16, 1866. On that day, he introduced the new governor of New Mexico before the Palace in Santa Fe:

My official term as governor of this Territory will expire at 12 o'clock this day, and it is with the greatest pleasure that I now have the honor of presenting and introducing to your acquaintance my successor to the executive chair, in the person of General Robert B. Mitchell. . . .[42]

Less than a month later, August 12, 1866, Connelly died in Santa Fe after a short illness. The funeral rites were performed by Bishop Jean B. Lamy in the Cathedral of Santa Fe. Connelly was buried in the chapel of San Rosario Cemetery in Santa Fe.

Henry Connelly had served New Mexico in a perilous time, and had left the territory in a more settled state than he had found it.

NOTES

1. *Territorial Papers of the U.S. Department of State,* New Mexico, Jan. 2, 1861—Dec. 23, 1864, National Archives, Washington.

2. Statements by Julian Henry Connelly, Jr., grandson of Henry Connelly, in personal interviews with the author, Sept.-Dec. 1958.

3. Ralph E. Twitchell, *The Leading Facts of New Mexican History,* v. II, Cedar Rapids, Torch, 1912.

4. John T. Hughes, *Doniphan's Expedition, Containing an Account of the Conquest of New Mexico,* Cincinnati, J. A. & V. P. James, 1850.

5. Ralph E. Twitchell, *The History of the Military Occupation of the Territory of New Mexico, from 1846 to 1851 by the Govt. of the United States,* Denver, Smith-Brooks, 1909.

6. P. St. George Cooke, *The Conquest of New Mexico and California; an Historical and Personal Narrative,* New York, Putnam's Sons, 1878.

7. *Ibid.*

8. Hubert Howe Bancroft, *History of Arizona and New Mexico, 1530-1888,* Denver, Smith-Brooks, 1909.

9. Hughes, *op. cit.*

10. *U.S. War Department, Letters sent,* Military affairs, 1800-1861, National Archives, Washington.

11. "Santa Fe in Notes and Documents," *The New Mexico Historical Review,* v. XXVI, Jan. 1950.

12. Stella M. Drumm (ed.), *Down the Santa Fe Trail and into Mexico, The Diary of Susan Shelby Magoffin, 1846-1847,* New Haven, Yale Univ. Press, 1926.

13. Ralph E. Twitchell, *Old Santa Fe; the Story of New Mexico's Ancient Capital* (ed. and trans. by R. E. Twitchell), Santa Fe, New Mexico Publishing Corp., 1925.

14. *Territorial Papers of the U.S. Department of State, op. cit.*

15. *Ibid.*

16. *Ibid.*

17. William I. Waldrip, "New Mexico During the Civil War," (unpublished Master's thesis, University of New Mexico, 1950).

18. *Territorial Papers of the U.S. Department of State, op. cit.*

19. *Ibid.*

20. Waldrip, *op. cit.*

21. Statements by Julian Henry Connelly, Jr., *op. cit.*

22. *Territorial Papers of the U.S. Department of State, op. cit.*

23. F. S. Donnell, "When Las Vegas was the Capital of New Mexico," *The New Mexico Historical Review*, v. VIII, Oct. 1933.

24. *Territorial Papers of the U.S. Department of State, op. cit.*

25. *Union Army Operations in the Southwest, Final Victory*, (from the official records, ed. by publishers), Albuquerque, Horn & Wallace, 1961.

26. *Territorial Papers of the U.S. Department of State, op. cit.*

27. *Ibid.*

28. *Ibid.*

29. *Union Army Operations, op. cit.*

30. *Territorial Papers of the U.S. Department of State, op. cit.*

31. *Ibid.*

32. *Territorial Papers of the U.S. Department of State, op. cit.*, Jan. 6, 1865—March 15, 1871.

33. *The Robert Todd Lincoln Collection of the Papers of Abraham Lincoln* (1790-1916), National Archives, Washington.

34. *Executive Documents Printed by Order of the House of Representatives during the First Session of the 38th Congress*, 1863-64, v. III, Nos. 41-42.

35. *Territorial Papers of the U.S. Department of State, op. cit.*, Jan. 2, 1861-Dec. 23, 1864.

36. *Ibid.*

37. *Ibid.*

38. *Ibid.*

39. *Ibid.*

40. *Ibid.*

41. *Territorial Papers of the U.S. Department of State, op. cit.*, Jan. 6, 1865—March 15, 1871.

42. *Ibid.*

ROBERT B. MITCHELL

SIX

Embattled Period

ROBERT B. MITCHELL

1866-69

A GROUP OF DIGNITARIES GATHERED UNDER THE PORTAL of the Palace of the Governors in Santa Fe on a clear Monday in mid-July of 1866. At the center of the group, a tall man rested his left hand on the Bible and raised his right hand in a solemn pledge. He was Robert B. Mitchell, being sworn in as the new territorial governor of New Mexico. The large crowd gathered before the Palace to hear his first remarks.

In the Santa Fe *Gazette,* July 21, 1866, appeared this comment: "The procession was one of the largest of the kind we have ever seen in Santa Fe and was an excellent index to the feeling which animated our people on the occasion."

Outgoing Governor Connelly expressed pleasure in President Andrew Johnson's choice, saying: "His brilliant record as a statesman, patriot and soldier, is familiar to us all. . . ."[1]

Mitchell's bearing was dignified, his words lofty, as he addressed the crowd:

> . . . New Mexico requires that every citizen shall use his personal and official influence to hasten the development

of its agricultural resources and mineral wealth. Your mountains from north to south, from east to west, are sealed treasures of uncoined gold and silver, whose keys are in the hands of a future now near at hand. . . .

Next to your mineral wealth in importance are your advantages for growing wool and manufacturing it into goods required for home consumption. . . .

You should early lay the foundation of a state in a thorough system of education. Without such education there is no permanent good. It alone endures and crowns a people with blessings and everlasting benefits. . . .[2]

Although it could not be apparent at his inauguration, Robert B. Mitchell was to become one of the most controversial governors in New Mexico's history—a governor whom the territorial legislature, eighteen months later, would petition the President of the United States to remove from office.

Yet, during the term of Governor Mitchell, several events of major importance occurred that improved conditions in the territory. The records of Mitchell's three years in office—1866 to 1869—show more progress than was made in any comparable period of New Mexico history up to that time.

The background of Governor Mitchell, who was forty-three at the time of his appointment, was excellent for his new position. In his native Ohio, he had studied and practiced law at Mansfield, and had served as mayor of Mount Gilead in 1855. Subsequently, he and his young wife migrated to Kansas Territory where, in succeeding years, he served in the Kansas territorial legislature, as a delegate to the Kansas constitutional convention and, later, as territorial treasurer of Kansas.[3]

But Robert Mitchell's most outstanding record was

made as a soldier on the field of battle in the Mexican and Civil wars. As a lieutenant in the Mexican War, he was so severely wounded while storming Chapultepec, outside Mexico City, that he was reported dead. In the early days of the Civil War, he organized the Second Kansas Volunteer Infantry and became commanding officer, with the rank of colonel.

During his first encounter with Confederate troops at Wilson Creek, near Springfield, Missouri, on August 10, 1861, Mitchell, although critically wounded, displayed such outstanding bravery and devotion to duty that he was officially cited for bravery.[4]

The following spring, Mitchell received a commission as brigadier-general from President Lincoln on April 8, 1862, and, with his new rank and new troops, engaged in two major battles—Perryville, in Kentucky, where he commanded the Ninth Division and lost 509 men, and Chickamauga, where he was in charge of the Cavalry Corps of the Army of the Cumberland.[5]

By this time, General Mitchell was a tough, hardened fighter. His stern military attitude was demonstrated in 1863 when he arrested 350 men of his own Union cavalry and threatened to shoot them. When his superiors questioned him about the incident, Mitchell stood his ground, arguing that mutiny in the face of the enemy was not a light offense and that it might be necessary to make an example of some of the prisoners. The General did not find it necessary to shoot the mutinous troops, but this incident established him as an arrogant, unyielding leader whose command bordered on the despotic.

Less than a month after Governor Mitchell's inauguration he began traveling throughout the territory to inspect its mineral resources. He had stated in his inaugural address: "There is perhaps no country on the globe of the same extent where gold, silver, platinum, copper, iron, zinc and quicksilver are so abundant. . . ."[6] Governor Mitchell believed this, and he intended to confirm it.

The Santa Fe *Gazette* reported in August: "Gov. Mitchell has gone to the Gila Country and Southwest part of the Territory to the reputed rich gold and silver mines of that region. . . ." In September, he inspected the northern part of New Mexico.

On November 12, 1866, after making a quick survey of the mineral wealth of New Mexico, Governor Mitchell traveled to the eastern United States, less than a month before the scheduled convening of the territorial legislature. While the legislature was meeting in Santa Fe in December 1866, Governor Mitchell remained in the East, advertising the advantages New Mexico offered to enterprising immigrants.

Governor Mitchell had requested only thirty days' leave of absence, but while in the East he received a sixty-day extension and did not return to New Mexico until March 1, 1867. The legislature met in his absence, and W. F. M. Arny, the secretary of the territory, acted as both governor and secretary.

The legislators and the people of New Mexico gave little thought to Governor Mitchell's absence from the territory during the first legislative session after his inauguration, because they knew and trusted Arny. The Council unanimously requested that the President and the Secretary of State reappoint Arny as secretary of the territory.

Upon Mitchell's return to New Mexico in the spring of 1867, the Santa Fe *Gazette* of March 2 reported his description of a great windstorm near Maxwell:

The driver was blown from his seat and did not light on the ground until he had been borne about 40 feet from the stage. The coach had to be fastened to the ground by chains to preserve it in position. The storm continued about 12 hours.

Governor Mitchell stirred up his own storm by declaring illegal and invalid the laws passed by the legislature and signed by Acting Governor Arny in his absence. Mitchell claimed Arny was not the duly appointed secretary of the territory, and, therefore, had no authority to serve as acting governor. Perhaps there was some justification for Mitchell's claim. In 1866, the President appointed a new secretary of the territory, who was confirmed by the United States Senate, yet he never arrived in New Mexico to serve. Arny continued to serve as secretary.

All government appointments filled by Arny, and confirmed by the Council, were declared invalid by Mitchell. He ordered the offices vacated and appointed a new slate of officials. However, the Arny-appointed officials refused to vacate their positions.

Governor Mitchell's new attorney general, Charles P. Clever, provided legal backing for the declarations of invalidity: "The acts performed by him [Arny] either as Acting Governor or as Secretary of the Territory, so far as they affect the rights and interests of the people thereof, are null and void."[7]

So began one of the most bitter political battles in New Mexico, which involved leading newspapers, candidates for Congress, and the legislature. It possibly contributed to the death of a chief justice of the New Mexico Supreme Court.

Despite Governor Mitchell's objections and declarations, Congress approved the acts of Acting Governor Arny and the legislature. On March 26, Congress resolved:

> . . . that the laws passed by the legislative assembly
> of the Territory of New Mexico . . . shall have the same
> force and effect as though the same had been approved and
> signed by the governor duly appointed. . . .[8]

New Mexico presently had a dual set of officers—those
appointed by Arny and confirmed by the Council, and the
new ones appointed by Governor Mitchell. The Arny-appointed attorney general wrote Mitchell:

> A few hours after your arrival from [the] states on last
> Tuesday, in your haste to annul the acts of the Legislative
> Council and the Governor you had left in charge, you sent
> me a verbal message that my resignation would be accepted,
> which I did not tender. Personally, I assure you, I was as
> anxious as yourself not to occupy a position which would
> necessarily bring me in contact with you officially. . . .[9]

But he did not resign.

Governor Mitchell was criticized by newspapers
throughout 1867. In the columns of the Santa Fe *New Mexican,* December 1, 1866, these questions were asked:

> What was Mitchell commissioned Governor of New
> Mexico for? . . . Governor Mitchell going to Washington
> ostensibly to 'greatly benefit' the Territory, but in reality to
> sell stock in bogus gold mines, is the sweetest specimen of
> serene impudence we have seen. Why did he in such an
> inglorious manner desert the gubernatorial chair and shirk
> the responsibilities incident to the office just on the eve of
> the meeting of the legislature?

He was accused in the same *New Mexican* article of
making his trip to Washington to sell "some gingerbread

titles to mines which were located by him and other persons when on his flying trip to the South shortly after his induction to the chair of state." Mitchell did not deny the accusation.

The *New Mexican* of May 4, 1867, contained an article attacking Mitchell for attempting to appoint John S. Watts to fill a vacancy in Congress: "We presume the people of New Mexico are no longer likely to feel the least surprise at any of Gov. Robert B. Mitchell's fantastic capers. . . . Bobby, however, assumes to override not only the representatives of the people, but the people themselves."

The same newspaper, on May 25, 1867, carried an editorial entitled: "What Gov. Mitchell has done for New Mexico." The editorial listed seven charges, such as setting up a party to influence the election of legislators, ingloriously leaving the territory, insulting the people by removing officers selected and chosen by the people, and several more. The editorial concluded with the question, "Should we not at once take some steps to relieve ourselves of his odious presence?"

After a year of smoldering revolt, the legislature convened in Santa Fe on December 2, 1867. The governor was discreet in his opening address to the legislature:

> I would most respectfully but earnestly recommend to your honorable bodies, the establishment of a liberal system of free schools throughout the territory and the levying of a sufficient tax on the property of the different counties to bring the law into effect and continue it in successful operation. We have today, within the boundaries of this Territory, one hundred and twenty thousand souls, and are without a single free school to educate a single child in the broad expanse of this Territory.

Messrs. Kronig and Co. have erected a fine woolen fac-
tory in the County of Mora, and are now in full and successful operation in the manufacture of all the different
woolen fabrics known in such establishments.

We have found gold in the 'Placers' and in the quartz
in inexhaustible quantities; our 'Placers' are now being
successfully worked in Pinos Altos, at the 'Placers' twenty-
five miles south of this city; at the Morena mines near Maxwell in the County of Mora, and other places. . . .

The *New Mexican* located in his address one paragraph
that had been lifted, word for word, from the legislative address of Governor Henry Connelly of 1865. Without giving
credit to Connelly, Mitchell quoted Connelly's paragraph
on agriculture:

. . . agriculture will be invested with new life, and
will be pursued, not only as an ordinary art within the reach
of the dullest and most ordinary intellect, but will be studied
and pursued as a science of the very highest and most useful order. That great improvements have been made, and
can still be made in the art of agriculture, must be admitted by all.

The *New Mexican* of December 17, 1867, printed the
two identical paragraphs, from Henry Connelly's address
and Robert Mitchell's, side by side, for comparison, and said
in an editorial: "We regret that Gov. Mitchell did not at
least clothe ideas of his predecessor in language of his own.
For, say what we will, we have some respect for the Gubernatorial office still left."

Legislative leaders chose two basic issues on which to
differ with Governor Mitchell. First, they refused to recognize the territorial officials appointed by Mitchell. Second,

the leaders planned to memorialize Congress, asking for a change in the Organic Act which gave an absolute veto to the governor. The measures, designed to take some of the powers away from the governor, passed both Houses unanimously.

Governor Mitchell promptly vetoed the memorial to Congress!

The legislature, the newspapers, and the people were inflamed. The *New Mexican* of January 7, 1868, expressed this opinion:

> A greater insult—a more despotic act—was never perpetrated upon a whole people than this conduct the Governor exhibits toward the whole population of New Mexico through their representatives . . . the sacred right of petition has been invaded in the most ruthless, uncalled for, and anti-republican manner.
>
> The right of petition is a sacred American right. The humblest American citizen may petition Congress for a redress of any grievance. This right of a territorial legislature to memorialize, or petition Congress, is a recognized right. . . . This then, the issue is a fairly made up one, as between the people of this Territory, who are free, and Gov. Robert B. Mitchell, the tyrant, who would enslave them. There is not a monarch on earth who does not recognize the right of the people, either directly or by their representatives, to petition the throne.

The legislature selected a "veto committee" to determine what should be done. This special committee consisted of one House member from each county. The committee reported on January 21, 1868:

> Your committee has therefore decidedly come to the following conclusion: that the official course of Gov.

Mitchell has been so gross and illegal in many of its parts
as to render him an object of aversion to the masses of our
people, instead of their true friend; and that the time has
arrived when his power to do good among our people has
entirely passed; when the occupation of the executive chair
can be considered by us as an imposition upon our people,
who are ignorant of having committed any crime where-
fore they should be punished. Therefore your committee
most respectfully submits the following joint resolution:

"Resolved, that the exercise of an unauthorized and
not delegated power, by the illegal acts of an unwarranted
assumption of legislative prerogatives, and for the attempt
to obstruct the will of the people of New Mexico, when
they desired through their legislature to appeal to the Congress of the United States for the redress of their grievances,
Gov. Robert B. Mitchell has made himself unworthy of the
executive seat of this Territory, and that this Legislative
Assembly respectfully urges upon the President of the
United States the early, if not the immediate, removal of the
present Governor of New Mexico." [10]

Both houses of the legislature approved the resolution,
the House by a vote of 17 to 5 and the Council by a vote of
8 to 3.

Gen. H. H. Heath, who had arrived in New Mexico
to replace Arny as secretary of the territory, sided with the
legislature in its fight with Governor Mitchell. It was apparently impossible to remain neutral in this political battle.

Although Governor Mitchell had bitter enemies, he had
ardent supporters. To dilute the effects of the legislature's
petition to the President for the removal of the governor, a
mass meeting of Mitchell's supporters was held in Santa Fe
on January 19, 1868, in the territorial library hall. The sup-

porters resolved that the removal of Governor Mitchell "would be a lasting and incalculable injury to our people and the Territory, because we earnestly believe that under his guidance our Territory will before long become a jewel in the crown of our country."

The resolution of the Mitchell supporters, sent to President Johnson, also condemned the legislature and Secretary Heath for their actions. It charged that legislators were unduly influenced by the secretary of the territory because he handled their per diem and mileage. The resolution asked for the immediate removal of Secretary Heath.

The legislature countered: "[Secretary Heath] is eminently worthy of the confidence of the entire people of New Mexico. . . ."[11]

The two Santa Fe newspapers took opposite views of the legislature. The *Weekly Gazette,* owned by Mitchell-appointed Attorney General C. P. Clever, blasted the adjourned legislature, on February 1, 1868:

> The Legislature adjourned on Thursday and the city is now free from the presence of that herd of notabilities that composed that body and which have made such striking exhibitions of their legislative ignorance and mental darkness during the last sixty days past.
>
> We trust that New Mexico will never again be represented in the capacity of lawmakers by such a combination of ignorance, prejudice, and dishonesty as that which has just adjourned after having by their puerile and factious proceedings disgraced the Territory and made the word, 'Legislator' a mockery and by-word in our midst. . . . Boys of ten years who should show as little intelligence as these legislators would be dismissed from any normal school in the country.

The *New Mexican,* February 4, 1868, on the other hand, defended the legislature:

> The Legislature, after an arduous service of 60 days, closed its labors last Thursday evening. . . .
> Never met a body of men more deeply imbued with a desire to do so much of good to the people than was this last one. . . . The session has, however, been a most important one in the history of New Mexico. To this Legislature the people owe eternal thanks for its fidelity to principle and its adhersion [sic] to their rights, and interests.

Secretary Heath had been granted a leave of absence, to take effect at the close of the legislative session. Governor Mitchell felt the need to tell his side of the story to friends in Washington. The governor and the territorial secretary could not both be absent from Santa Fe at the same time. Governor Mitchell falsely advised the State Department that Secretary Heath wished to decline his sixty-day leave. The State Department cancelled Heath's leave. Governor Mitchell, having succeeded in forcing Heath to remain in Santa Fe, was then free to go to Washington.

When Mitchell's leave was finished, he obtained an extension of several weeks by personal recommendation of President Johnson. Thus again he postponed Heath's departure from Santa Fe. This maneuver apparently succeeded, because President Johnson did not remove Mitchell from office, as the territorial legislature had requested. President Johnson may have been unwilling to act because Congress had recently passed the Tenure of Office Act which prevented the President from removing, without its approval, any government officer that had been confirmed by the Senate.

In August 1868, however, Congress did recognize the

vetoed memorial which had caused the break between Governor Mitchell and the legislature. Congress changed the Organic Act of New Mexico by limiting the governor's absolute veto power, and allowed any measure to pass over a gubernatorial veto by a two-thirds majority vote. This change considerably weakened the power of the governor and opened the way for the legislature to exercise greater control over territorial affairs.[12]

Modification of the Organic Act was doubtless a major victory for the legislature, but it also served to generate greater animosity between Governor Mitchell and that body. The bitter political battle spread to other quarters, causing a general atmosphere of anger, suspicion and intrigue in Santa Fe—even between friends.

More seriously, the division and consequent hostility between the parties may have indirectly brought about the violent death of John P. Slough, chief justice of the territorial Supreme Court.

Justice Slough had an exceptional command of abusive language, which he used masterfully and willingly against any opponent. He once used his verbal abuse on Governor Mitchell for having pardoned a man who had been sentenced in his court. For this action, he charged Governor Mitchell with violating his oath, ignorance of executive responsibility, and selling himself to improper influence.

Justice Slough's acid words apparently had been used on others. During the legislative session, Col. William L. Rynerson, a member of the Council, introduced a resolution censuring the judge. Justice Slough countered by calling Rynerson "A thief in the army, a thief out of the army, a coward and a S.O.B."[13] Those abusive words were uttered on Saturday, December 14, 1868.

The following afternoon, about one o'clock, Judge Slough arrived at a Santa Fe hotel for his usual Sunday lunch. Colonel Rynerson was waiting for him. A witness, Santiago L. Hubbell, described the events that followed in an article in the Santa Fe *New Mexican* on January 14:

> I saw Slough and Rynerson approaching each other, using angry words. . . . Rynerson demanded, "Judge, you spoke very harshly of me last night and you must retract your language. . . ."
>
> "I don't propose to take it back," retorted the Judge, "What are you going to do about it?" Again, Rynerson demanded the foul language be retracted. He threatened to shoot. The Judge, reaching for his pocket, yelled: "Then shoot, damn you!" Rynerson shot. The Judge fell dead.

Rynerson was tried before a San Miguel County jury and acquitted.

The Santa Fe *New Mexican,* March 24, 1868, summed up the matter: "Thus ends this case, and we congratulate Colonel Rynerson upon this issue." Rynerson was subsequently appointed adjutant-general of New Mexico and unanimously confirmed by the Council.

Governor Mitchell's problems continued to accumulate. The territorial treasury was bankrupt. The tax collections totaled $15,650 for the year ending November 15, 1868, and expenditures were $32,679, making a deficit of $17,029. Governor Mitchell spoke about money matters:

> A system of equal taxation must be adopted, and the sooner the Legislature takes hold of this subject and settles it satisfactorily, the better it will be for the Territory. Our credit must be redeemed. Our paper is depreciated. . . .[14]

On December 22, 1868, the *New Mexican* directed attention to financial matters:

[Let us have an investigation] of the enormous extrav-
agance and wastefulness of Mitchell's administration, that
spends over $30,000 a year of the people's money, leaving
their Treasury bankrupt to the tune of some $17,000 and
the people themselves not a whit the better for it.

What has Mitchell and Co. done with all this money?
Let the Legislature appoint a special committee to determine the question.

On July 10, 1869, a *New Mexican* editorial said:

When the legislature met last winter, Territorial
Treasurer warrants were worth no more than fifty cents on
the dollar. By the time the august body adjourned, warrants
had dropped in value to twenty-five cents on the dollar.
They cannot be sold for more than that amount.

At the close of the legislative session, February 6, 1869,
the Santa Fe *Gazette,* a pro-Mitchell paper, again attacked
the legislature as it had done the year before:

The Legislature has adjourned and the Lord be praised
therefor. Santa Fe breathes easy, the atmosphere being puri-
fied by the riddance of the nuisance with which we have
been infected during the last sixty days. Some may think
the figure put in strong colors, but it is, nevertheless, a
faithful one, as will be testified by any honest observer of
events as they have been passing. . . .

Who does not know that those who controlled both
houses of the recent legislature were in the market for sale?
That the fate of measures was decided by the price paid for
them. Don't squirm. There is the truth.

Another event of 1868 repeated itself in 1869. Again
Governor Mitchell out-maneuvered Secretary Heath and
prevented him from taking leave. On February 4, 1869, just

one week before Heath's leave was to begin, Governor
Mitchell informed him that he would be leaving at once.
The governor had permission for leave dated December 11,
1868, which he had not used. And so Governor Mitchell,
driving a two-wheeled cart, departed for Washington. He
thus deprived Heath of another opportunity to secure ad-
ministrative and Congressional support for his faction.

Heath complained to the Secretary of State:

> The fact, however, is that Governor Mitchell has not
> availed himself of the leave granted: but has, on this day,
> when but six full days of his leave remained to him, and
> with the full official knowledge that you had granted me
> 'two months' leave from the day on which his expired, left
> this city for Washington; thus absolutely barring me of my
> right under the leave granted by you. . . .[15]

Mitchell remained in Washington for some weeks, visiting important officials. Then, on March 30, Mitchell ten-
dered his resignation to the President, "to take effect from
the date of the qualification of my successor."[16]

On April 3, President Ulysses S. Grant appointed Col.
C. C. Crowe, formerly of the Confederate Army, to become
governor of New Mexico. Colonel Crowe failed to qualify
after his confirmation was delayed for a long period of time.
Mitchell returned to New Mexico on May 24, still governor.
Secretary Heath, informed of Mitchell's resignation, tele-
graphed for instructions: "Is Mitchell to be recognized
Governor? He has returned."

The Secretary of State informed Heath that the Organic
Act provided that "he shall hold his office for four years, and
until his successor shall be appointed and qualified, unless
sooner removed by the President."[17]

Governor Mitchell's last official act as New Mexico's chief executive clearly reflected his arbitrary attitude—he declared war on the Gila Apaches and Navajos by executive proclamation. This action brought a resounding protest from Congress, the State Department, the U.S. Army, and his own official family.

Mitchell's unsupported declaration of war probably caused the President and Congress to move rapidly in choosing his successor. On August 16, 1869, the Honorable William A. Pile arrived in Santa Fe as the new governor of New Mexico. One of Pile's first official acts was to modify the war proclamation issued by Mitchell.

After being relieved as governor, Mitchell remained in New Mexico to attend to his mining interests. On March 22, 1870, he left New Mexico. He went first to Kansas and later to Washington. He died in 1882 and was buried in the Congressional cemetery.

Despite Governor Mitchell's continuous political battles with both territorial secretaries and with the legislature, his administration saw some progress. The approach of the railroad to within 180 miles of New Mexico was one important event of the period. Telegraph lines were completed and brought New Mexico into telegraphic communication with the entire civilized world. The governor was also able to report: "We have secured from the government a daily mail route. . . . There has also been established a daily stage line from Maxwell's Ranch at the crossing of the Cimarron to Virginia City and Elizabethtown. . . ."[18]

New Mexico's peonage system was abolished during the administration of Governor Mitchell by an act of Congress.

It is difficult to determine how any progress could have been made when the branches of territorial government were at such bitter odds. Certainly there was no spirit of cooperation between the executive and legislative arms of the territorial government. Even so, Governor Robert B. Mitchell's embattled term did see progress. But the old wounds had to be healed, and much remained to be done.

N O T E S

1. *Territorial Papers of the U.S. Department of State,* New Mexico, Jan. 6, 1865—March 15, 1871, National Archives, Washington.

2. *Ibid.*

3. W. A. Mitchell, "Historic Linn," (from *La Cyge Weekly Journal, Collections of the Kansas State Historical Society,* 1923-25, ed. by William Elsey Connelly), Topeka, Kansas State, 1925.

4. *The War of the Rebellion: A Compilation of the Official Records of the Union and Confederate Armies,* Series 1, v. III, Washington, Government Printing Office, 1880.

5. *Ibid.*

6. *Territorial Papers of the U.S. Department of State, op. cit.*

7. *Ibid.*

8. Santa Fe *New Mexican,* April 20, 1867.

9. *Territorial Papers of the U.S. Department of State, op. cit.*

10. Santa Fe *New Mexican,* January 21, 1868.

11. *Territorial Papers of the U.S. Department of State, op. cit.*

12. Santa Fe *New Mexican,* Aug. 11, 1868.

13. Santa Fe *New Mexican,* Jan. 14. 1868.

14. *Territorial Papers of the U.S. Department of State, op. cit.*

15. *Ibid.*

16. *Ibid.*

17. *Ibid.*

18. *Ibid.*

WILLIAM A. PILE

SEVEN

Battle of the Archives

WILLIAM A. PILE

1869-71

ILLIAM A. PILE, FORMER METHODIST MINISTER, congressman, and army officer, became the seventh territorial governor of New Mexico on August 16, 1869. The next day, the Santa Fe *Weekly New Mexican* reported: "The inauguration of General Pile, yesterday, as Governor of New Mexico, was a very pleasant affair. . . . The preference indicated by him for a plain businesslike way of taking possession of the Executive office, may, we think, be regarded [as indicating] an intelligent, judicious, and vigorous administration."

During the fall of 1869, Governor Pile applied himself to analyzing the problems of New Mexico. He spoke to influential citizens, traveled over the state and studied the state's background. He appraised New Mexico on September 18, 1869:

> For a number of years the conditions of this Territory have been very unsatisfactory, life and property has [sic] been insecure, industry has languished, production has not advanced; and there has been no material increase in the population or wealth of the Territory. . . .

With an area of seventy seven thousand square miles, a population of 100,000 souls, a climate unsurpassed and unsurpassable, abundant mineral resources and grazing, qualities superior to any other portion of the Union—with all these and more there has been no increase in population or wealth within the last ten years and at this hour your Territorial Treasury is bankrupt, the administration of civil government imperfect, no attempt is made toward the general education of your children . . . and every branch of industry and business is languishing and stagnant. Beyond doubt there is a crisis in the affairs of the Territory. Unless something is done speedily to remedy the present state of things, public officers paid in worthless scrip in increasing numbers will resort to speculation and corruption. . . . What is to be done?

Let all the people arise from their indifference and lethargy and by a wise and prudent policy vigorously and perseveringly carried out, secure to themselves and their posterity the blessings of good government and prosperity.[1]

Governor Pile began working on a legislative program and an executive administration to set New Mexico on a proper course. He quickly decided that the most urgent problem was the fiscal plight of the territory. He said:

Something should and must be done to repair the credit of the Territory. I think the existing debt (say $60,000) ought to be funded in a ten year bond at the lowest possible interest; and I cannot see how the government of the Territory is to be maintained without some system of equal and just taxation.[2]

The value of territorial warrants had dropped to twenty-five cents on the dollar. They were purchased primarily to pay fines and license fees; thus, revenues for the territory consisted of twenty-five cent territorial warrants paid to the territory at dollar face value. No actual money had been paid into the treasury for a two-year period. Governor Pile reported this state of affairs to Secretary of State Hamilton Fish.[3]

The territorial legislature met in December 1869. Under the domination of the governor, the legislature enacted the first general property tax in the history of the territory. The tax provided twenty cents on each hundred dollars of valuation for territorial purposes, and five cents for county purposes. With a few exceptions, the tax was levied upon all real and personal property in the territory. The tax law, ending the constant financial crises in New Mexico, was signed January 24, 1870.

The legislature also modified the existing license law covering all persons engaged in businesses or professions. The new measure, moderate and fair, was modeled after a United States law.

The legislature followed another suggestion of the governor and funded all outstanding warrants, issued and dated previous to May 1, 1870, in bonds payable in ten years but redeemable at the pleasure of the territory. The bonds carried a ten percent interest rate. Territorial warrants rose from twenty-five cents to fifty cents on the dollar within two hours after the measure was approved by the legislature, reported the Santa Fe *Weekly New Mexican* on February 8, 1870.

While the governor was preoccupied with the major problems of the office during the first part of 1870, he committed the greatest blunder of his career—and all of New Mexico became indignant about it.

The blunder of Governor Pile's administration—the one event best remembered by all historians—was the partial destruction of the archives of New Mexico. For this act, Gov-

ernor Pile was charged with being a pig-headed drunkard
and a political dead beat. He was charged by men who could
not even spell his name with "using many of these valuable
documents for kindling the fires in his office and sold cart-
loads of others for waste paper."[4]

The events of April and May 1870, were colored by
political charges exchanged by the pro- and anti-Pile factions. The "battle of the archives" began April 2, 1870,
when the Santa Fe *Weekly Post,* an anti-Pile newspaper,
charged that Governor Pile's appointed librarian and
friend, Ira M. Bond, had sold and destroyed some of the
valuable archives of the territory.

Librarian Bond attempted to answer in the Santa Fe
New Mexican, April 6, what he called "false and malicious"
charges. Bond, at first, took no responsibility for the papers.
He claimed that they had never been placed in his care or in
the care of the library. He also asserted that a certain "paper-
filled room" contained refuse and worthless papers, not valuable archives:

> I have ascertained from several of our oldest, most in-
> telligent and leading native "families" that these papers
> were carefully examined by two of our former secretaries,
> who were well acquainted with the Spanish language, and
> what were worth preserving were carefully put up in
> bundles, and placed in boxes, which are now in the secre-
> tary's office, and the papers spoken of were considered as
> refuse matter and worthless papers, and were thrown in—
> apparently through the windows—on to the dirt floor of an
> unused side room, and Governor Pile in repairing, clean-
> ing up and placing the Palace in decent order, found these
> papers in the way, and wanting to clean up and use the
> room immediately ordered me to have them removed,
> which after again looking over them, I did. . . .[5]

Governor Pile seems to have become the central figure in the controversy by ordering the paper-filled room cleaned to make an office for Attorney General Thomas Catron. Later, however, Catron stated in the Albuquerque *Republican Review,* May 7, 1870, that Pile "never gave me permission to occupy it nor attempted to exercise any control whatever over it."

Librarian Bond, after discussing the problem with the governor, attempted to recover all of the missing documents. In a statement of April 6, he said: "I have got the papers back and propose to keep them until next winter, and ask the legislature to appoint a committee to examine them, and preserve any of them that they think proper. I venture the assertion that there will not be one pound of them preserved. . . ."[6]

Ira Bond's inconsistency hurt the governor. After asserting April 6 that all the archives had been returned, he later advertised in the Santa Fe newspaper for the return of the missing archives. He also took a new position on the value of the documents in the paper-filled room. His advertisement read: "All persons having any of the papers recently removed from the Palace, in their possession are notified that they were removed by mistake as to their value; and all such persons are requested to return them at once to the Territorial library."[7]

Librarian Bond issued yet another statement in an effort to establish that the missing papers were worthless and that the governor was not responsible for their removal:

It was the universal opinion of all people that ever looked at the papers in the room that they were worthless refuse matter. . . .

I then to get the papers out of the way, and supposing them worthless, sold them to Mr. Wendell Debus without the knowledge of the Governor. Mr. Debus paid thirty dollars for the papers.

Within a day or two, complaint was made to the Governor . . . and he sent for me and directed the recovery of the papers.

I went to Mr. Debus and told him not to dispose of any of them, nor to use them, that I wanted them back and would let the next Legislature dispose of them as they thought proper. . . . they are now safely preserved in the hall of the Legislative part of the Palace. . . .

A few papers which got into other hands have not yet been recovered but every possible means are being made by the Governor and myself to recover them.[8]

The citizens of Santa Fe and Albuquerque were not satisfied that all of the archives had been returned. With Judge Kirby Benedict as chairman, a mass meeting was called April 16, in Santa Fe, to "ascertain who is responsible for said destruction. . . ." A committee of six, with Jesús M. Sena y Baca as chairman, was appointed to investigate and report on the archives.

A similar meeting, held in Albuquerque on April 19, adopted resolutions approving the investigation: "The committee appointed at the meeting in Santa Fe are respectfully requested to make a strict and thorough investigation into all the circumstances connected with said destruction of public records, and make a full report of the same."[9]

The Santa Fe committee reported on April 23. The report stated that the archives of New Mexico had been well preserved for two centuries; that recently the archives had been placed in an unfurnished room, where they were not being injured or wasted, that Governor Pile desired the use of the room. The report continued:

. . . Governor W. A. Pile . . . gave instructions to
the Librarian, Mr. Ira Bond, to have them removed, which
was done, into an open out-house, unfit for the protection of
anything of value; . . . the said Governor Pile . . . gave
a portion thereof to the convict prisoners to be used as they
might desire, and the residue thereof compelled Mr. Bond
to dispose of, under a threat of consuming them by fire if
they were not taken out of the way, which were thereupon
sold by the said Librarian, and a portion of them have
thereby become entirely lost.[10]

The report was received by the committee. A drafting
committee of four citizens was appointed to draft resolutions
expressive of the sense of the meeting. The committee retired
and in about twenty minutes reported. The preamble of the
report accused the governor of being "the prime cause of the
sale and destruction of said archives, having himself given
away a portion of them, and under peremptory instructions
to the Librarian, Ira M. Bond, compelled him to dispose of
the residue."

Then followed resolutions expressing the greatest possible censure upon a governor:

Resolved, That in the estimation of this meeting the
outrage upon enlightenment and civilization committed by
the said William A. Pile, he having thus destroyed the
archives of the country, is unsurpassed in history and
equaled only in the barbarous burning of the libraries of
Alexandria.

Resolved, That the said William A. Pile . . . has
proven himself unworthy of the confidence of our people
and unfit to occupy amongst us any position of honor, trust,
or profit. . . .

Resolved, That the President of the United States be
and is hereby respectfully solicited to remove the said Wil-

liam A. Pile from the position he now occupies as Governor
of the Territory, which office he is not capacitated to fill,
and which he has, by his conduct, disgraced.

The preamble and resolutions were unanimously adopted.[11]

For years, the archives continued to return to the territorial library. Librarian J. C. McKenzie, in 1872, publicly
acknowledged the "receipt of some very ancient and valuable
Spanish papers (part of the old archives of New Mexico),
from Thomas Coghlan. . . . I have heard of many more of
these papers among our citizens, and should be glad if the
parties holding them would follow Mr. Coghlan's public
spirited example."[12]

The Santa Fe *Weekly New Mexican* commended Mr.
Coghlan and asked those who obtained the archives for little
or nothing "through a blunder which met with the severest
censure from all parts of the country" to return them to the
library.[13] Additional papers were returned as late as March
4, 1886, by Eluterio Barela.

The partial destruction and dispersal of the archives in
1870 is the most famous act of Pile's administration.

Additional opposition, possibly unwarranted, plagued
Governor Pile. A Republican, he was accused of making a
bargain with New Mexico Democrats whereby he would gain
their support for a seat in the United States Senate if New
Mexico were granted statehood. His enemies asserted that
he had agreed to split state offices with the Democrats in return for their support.

Governor Pile wrote his denial to President Grant:

If such accusations are based on movement in this Territory to form a state government, I can establish beyond
question that such movement only contemplated uniting
all the friends of the movement in its favor, and no sacrifice

of principle or division of office. . . . I refer to this for the reason I can think of nothing else upon which accusations against me can be founded. . . .[14]

Sentiment was favorable in New Mexico, and divided throughout the nation, on the granting of statehood to New Mexico. The Chicago *Evening Journal,* May 3, 1870, commented:

> The Territory needs two things, first riddance of Indians; second, a railroad. At present the isolation from society, using the term broadly, is so effectual that no man of sense and sanity would go there to settle. . . .

The New York *Times,* February 10, 1871:

> Here, upon the plains, in the heart of our worst civilization, is an American city 300 years old . . . seventy miles south is Albuquerque, younger, but with all the signs of ignorance and sloth.

Permanent progress toward solution of the Indian problem was achieved by Governor Pile. He mentioned in his opening address that "bands of lawless savages roam over your soil plundering citizens." During his administration, a firm policy was maintained toward the Indians.

On August 24, 1869, Pile issued a General Order, instructing the probate judges to form posses in each precinct up to twenty-four men to punish and drive off marauding bands of Indians. Posses were formed in twelve frontier counties to pursue and, if necessary, exterminate all marauding bands of Indians off their reservations.

Guns and ammunition were issued from the Governor's Palace to citizens for use by the posses. The governor also impressed the armed citizens with their responsibilities. He wanted rigorous measures used to suppress the Indian outrages, but he cautioned the posses to use great care: "The President is very apprehensive that those citizens, so organized, will commit excesses and abuses, and only consents allowing a continuance of this policy because of his confidence in my intention and ability to control them."[15]

Because of the carefully supervised action of the posses, the first six months of 1870 were the most peaceful since the American occupation. Not a single white man was murdered by the Indians and there was very little loss of stock. Nor was there a single complaint of abuse by armed citizens. The last six months were also relatively peaceful, marking an excellent year in New Mexico.[16]

In the Santa Fe *Weekly New Mexican*, November 2, 1870, appeared this comment on Governor Pile's Thanksgiving Proclamation: "The past year has been one of bountiful harvests and healthful skies, of peace and prosperity for which we ought to be profoundly thankful. . . ."

During the first part of 1871, the Indians in Grant County got out of hand. "About twenty men and women have been murdered and horribly mutilated within the last three weeks," Governor Pile wrote the Secretary of State.[17]

Governor Pile left Santa Fe for Silver City on May 1, 1871, to be sure that harsh and illegal measures were not taken by the armed and aroused citizens. He was received warmly, and the Silver City newspaper stated that the people of that place would rather see Governor Pile than the President.

The governor was able to prevent hasty action by citizens, and he strengthened the garrisons and posses to bring the situation under control.

Even though there was some trouble in the southwest and with the Comanches and Kiowas along the Texas plains, the posse policy under Governor Pile proved workable. The

Utes and Jicarilla Apaches in the north were quiet. The
Navajos were relatively peaceful and the Mescalero Apaches
in the southeast were not troublesome.

Citizens had been selling ammunition to, and purchas-
ing stolen property from, the Indians. Often whisky was exchanged to the Indians for stolen cattle. Pile firmly halted
this illegal trading between Indians and whites.

William Pile entered into all phases of New Mexico's
social and economic life. He became president of the Santa
Fe Bible Society, lectured on "Courage, the Measure of a
Man's Power," and also on the evils of alcohol. He was called
an eloquent orator and a sound and vigorous thinker. The
forty-year-old ex-minister filled the pulpit of the Presbyterian
church in Santa Fe. He and his wife entertained at a formal
reception at the Palace which was reported in the *Weekly
New Mexican,* February 1, 1870.

Governor Pile actively engaged in business in New
Mexico. He helped to organize the Santa Fe Artesian Well
and Mining Company. It was formed "for the purpose of
sinking an artesian well which was to supply that rich section
of our country with sufficient water for mineral, agricultural
and pastural purposes."[18]

Pile cautioned New Mexico business men about the
fallacy of building an economy based upon government ex-
penditure:

> The key to the utter want of enterprise in our Terri-
> tory can be found in its entire dependency on government
> patronage ever since its annexation to the United States.
> . . . We had become so used to counting on the sale of our
> produce at a good price to the government, that the idea of
> a change never entered our thought and we believed that
> we had a right to demand of government that this state of
> affairs should continue forever. . . .

Our Civil War closed leaving us a tremendous debt to pay, which naturally had the tendency to curtail expenses in every department of government. The demand for grain, our chief dependency, became limited. New Mexico in 1847 had far more resources than it has today.

We tried to build up New Mexico, depending on government expenditures as our source of wealth, and the very hour our accustomed supply of government drafts fell short, we went back to where we found it 22 years ago, less the then existing resources.[19]

Governor Pile allied himself with Lucien B. Maxwell and became vice-president of the Maxwell Land Grant and Railway Company. The huge grant, consisting of two million acres of land, became known throughout the U.S. with the discovery of gold in the Moreno Valley in 1867. Prior to that time, Maxwell had ignored the presence of squatters on his land. Now he asserted ownership and demanded royalty on the claims taken upon the grant. Some recognized Maxwell's rights, others did not. The question divided the people of Colfax County into two groups—the "grant" party, and the "anti-grant" party. The "grant" men were employed by the Maxwell Land Grant and Railway Company, and the "anti-grant" men were the small homesteaders and ranchers and miners. Governor Pile, as a director in the company, placed his influence squarely behind the "grant" faction.[20]

On April 15, 1871, he went to Cimarron where a serious dispute between the miners and the Company took place. He saw the Maxwell property near Elizabethtown taken by an armed mob during the month. On April 21, 1871, he issued a Governor's Proclamation:

Whereas, there is a state of lawlessness and violence in the vicinity of the quartz mills and gulch mining claims on Ute Creek in the County of Colfax. . . .

Whereas, persons claiming and working gulch mining claims in the locality above mentioned have unlawfully and riotously combined together for the purpose of resisting the employees of the said Maxwell Land Grant and Railway Co. from entering upon and working mines claimed and owned by said Co. . . .

Now, therefore, I, William A. Pile do issue this, my Proclamation, forbidding the carrying of arms in violation of the law. . . .[21]

So Governor Pile, a director of the Company, entered the dispute between the Company and settlers and miners. He ordered the miners and settlers not to carry arms, eliminating their only weapon against the Company.

In May 1871, William A. Pile received word that he had been appointed United States Minister to Venezuela. Previously he had desired to become minister to Brazil and President Grant had nominated him for that position, but he was never confirmed by the United States Senate. He had settled for the governorship of New Mexico. Now he was to go to South America.

On June 3, 1871, as he was preparing to leave the territory, the governor placed some homely advertisements in the Santa Fe *New Mexican*:

ANYONE WISHING TO BUY A FIRST CLASS AMERICAN COW WITH YOUNG CALF CAN BE ACCOMMODATED BY CALLING ON THE GOVERNOR.

A VERY FINE PIANO. INQUIRE AT THE RESIDENCE OF THE GOVERNOR.

Governor Pile auctioned his household goods June 21, 1871, before the Palace. On June 26, he and his family left Santa Fe for the States, by way of Denver.

Pile served as minister to Venezuela until 1874. He moved to Monrovia, California, where he died July 7, 1889.

The Santa Fe *New Mexican* acclaimed his accomplishments, May 24, 1871, referring to him as "a gentleman of
unexceptionable deportment in private, business and social
relations. . . . We regret to hear of the appointment . . .
believing that we lose a valuable public officer. . . ."

Unfortunately, Governor Pile's solid accomplishments
in public finance and Indian control have been all but forgotten as historians recall the "blunder of 1870."

NOTES

1. *Territorial Papers of the U.S. Department of State,* New Mexico, Jan. 6, 1865—March 15, 1871, National Archives, Washington.

2. *Ibid.*

3. *Ibid.*

4. Lansing B. Bloom, ed., "Bourke on the Southwest," *The New Mexico Historical Review,* v. X, Oct. 1935.

5. Santa Fe *Daily New Mexican,* April 6, 1870.

6. *Ibid.*

7. Santa Fe *Daily New Mexican,* April 22, 1870.

8. Albuquerque *Republican Review,* May 7, 1870.

9. *Destruction of Spanish and Mexican Archives in New Mexico by United States Officials,* Bancroft Library, University of California, Berkeley.

10. *Ibid.*

11. *Ibid.*

12. Santa Fe *Weekly New Mexican,* Sept. 17, 1872.

13. *Ibid.*

14. J. Manuel Espinosa, "Memoir of a Kentuckian in New Mexico," *The New Mexico Historical Review,* v. XIII, Jan. 1938.

15. Santa Fe *Weekly New Mexican,* Nov. 2, 1869.

16. *Territorial Papers of the U.S. Department of State, op. cit.*

17. *Territorial Papers of the U.S. Department of State, op. cit.,* April 28, 1871—Nov. 16, 1872.

18. Santa Fe *Daily New Mexican,* June 16, 1871.

19. *Territorial Papers of the U.S. Department of State, op. cit.*

20. William A. Keleher, *Maxwell Land Grant, A New Mexico Item,* Santa Fe, Rydal, 1942.

21. Santa Fe *Daily New Mexican,* April 21, 1871.

MARSH GIDDINGS

EIGHT

Revolution in Santa Fe

MARSH GIDDINGS

1871-75

MARSH GIDDINGS, APPOINTED GOVERNOR OF NEW Mexico by President Ulysses S. Grant, was a partisan Republican from Michigan. He arrived in Santa Fe on September 1, 1871, not realizing that the bitterest legislative fight in the history of the territory would cloud his administration.

Governor Giddings enjoyed partisan politics, and was one "of the founders and honored champions of the Republican party," but partisan politics in New Mexico far surpassed any previous political experience of his career.[1]

In a letter to U.S. Secretary of State Hamilton Fish, September 1, 1871, Giddings enclosed this report by an eyewitness of an incident in Mesilla:

> The election excitement in this valley culminated today [August 27, 1871] in one of the most fearful affrays it has ever been my ill fortune to witness. It is no exaggeration to say that the plaza has been literally drenched with blood. At the present writing it is known that seven persons have been killed while the estimate of wounded reaches as high as thirty of whom seven or eight are wounded mortally. . . .

The republican and democratic parties had each
selected today as the most suitable time for the grand dem-
onstration of the campaign. . . . At five o'clock both lines
were marching through the plaza in a high state of excitement exchanging defiant *vivas,* when the sharp crack of a
pistol was heard and in a moment all was confusion. At this
time there must have been at least a thousand people in
the plaza. The first shot was quickly followed by others and
the firing at once became general. . . . The dead and
wounded fell upon all sides, and noncombatants hurried in
every direction for shelter. A courier has been sent to Fort
Selden for troops. . . .[2]

Governor Giddings, born in Litchfield County, Con-
necticut, in 1816, moved to Kalamazoo, Michigan, in 1831.
After passing the bar examination, he actively engaged in
politics, serving as a delegate to the national Republican
convention which nominated Abraham Lincoln. He was also
a delegate to the convention which nominated U. S. Grant, a
member of the constitutional convention in Michigan,
of the state legislature, of the electoral college, and a probate
judge. President Grant nominated Giddings to become con-
sul general to India. He declined this appointment but later
accepted appointment as governor of New Mexico.[3]

The new governor delivered his first address to the territorial legislature December 7, 1871:

I feel confident your honorable bodies, the Council and
the House, will heartily and energetically join the executive, and permit no plans or schemes for the personal ambition or gains of any individual to distract us from our sole
duty of working with an eye single to the general welfare
of the people of New Mexico.

Governor Giddings enumerated "some of the causes of slow progress in New Mexico—none in nearly a quarter of a century since becoming part of the United States." He listed lack of education, poor revenue laws, distance to railroads, confusion in Spanish land grant titles, huge state debt causing devaluation of warrants. He continued:

> New Mexico with a population of 113,000 and yet not a single common school of the character found in every other state and territory of the Republic of America . . . New Mexico claiming to be a civilized people exhibits the mournful fact that outside of Santa Fe there is scarcely a school of any kind whatever. . . .
>
> The Kansas Pacific Railroad now brings us to a point from which we can reach Santa Fe in three days by stage. . . .
>
> Laws for the consolidation as well as for condemning lands for rights of way over the grounds necessary for the construction of roads should be enacted. . . .
>
> A beginning could be made by a tax of one mill on the dollar. This would raise but little money compared to our needs. But it would be a beginning.

He spoke of the $74,000 state debt and recommended all taxes be paid in money instead of thirty-cent state warrants. He asked for a revision of the taxes on classes of labor.

He urged the establishment of a good library, and asked that the executive be placed in charge of it with power to appoint a librarian to hold office during the pleasure of the executive, and to receive a salary of $500 a year.[4]

All went well with the governor and the legislature until the introduction of a measure on December 30, 1871, assigning Chief Justice Joseph G. Palen from the first district in Santa Fe to the third district in Mesilla. The measure passed through both houses with unnecessary speed—without being printed, without a reference to a committee, and without time for any deliberation.

Stakes were high in the attempt to reassign Judge Palen. The Denver *Rocky Mountain News* stated, editorially:

> The cause of this action is two decisions made by the Chief Justice, and affirmed by the Supreme Court, which were inimical to a large and powerful money ring. The ring determined apparently to get rid of the Chief Justice. . . .[5]

The purpose of the reassignment, according to the Santa Fe *New Mexican,* January 2, 1872, was "to annoy, injure, and weaken the influence of Judge Palen."

Sides were drawn for or against Judge Palen. The executive veto power placed Governor Giddings in the middle of the controversy. A petition was circulated in Santa Fe pressuring the governor not to veto the measure. A subsequent Council report stated:

> The citizens of Santa Fe, irrespective of party, to the number of 400, including more than two-thirds of the members of both the Council and the House, addressed a petition to His Excellency the Governor respectfully requesting him not to interpose his veto as against the clearly expressed desire of the people of New Mexico. There can be no question whatever that it was the purpose of the bill alluded to to remove Joseph G. Palen, Chief Justice of the Territory, from the First Judicial District to the more remote Third Judicial District. . . .[6]

Governor Giddings delivered a strong veto message:

> Is it wise to open the door, in violation of a settled usage of more than 20 years, by which the intimidation of a judge may be attempted by holding over him the rod of a prospective legislative enactment to remove and disgrace

him at the caprice of the wealthy and influential bad men who would degrade the judiciary of the Territory to secure some selfish end? Under these circumstances I am impelled to return to you the bill without my approval.[7]

Governor Giddings' veto message sparked the most serious legislative revolution in the history of the territory. Although the vote to sustain the veto carried, 12 to 4, this was no indication of the strength of the opposition to Judge Palen. Even several of the leading Republicans conspired with House Democrats to override the sustained veto.

Their plan was to remove four Republican representatives elected from Taos County, and replace them with Democrats, and in the Council to remove one Republican and appoint a Democrat—thus giving the Democrats control of both chambers of the legislature.

This scheme was characterized by the Santa Fe *New Mexican*, January 5, 1872, as "a revolutionary program which, if successful, will shock the moral sense of every man of character and render unsecure in this Territory all the rights that men hold dear and sacred."

The action began on January 5, 1872, with Alejandro Branch moving to remove the four elected Taos Republican representatives and replace them with Democrats. On this date, the session was more than half finished. The motion carried, 14 to 8. The speaker appointed a committee of three "for the purpose of notifying the Hon. José Cordova, Mateo Romero, Juan B. Gonzales, and Francisco Antonio Montoya of their being entitled to seats as representatives of the county of Taos and to come forward to occupy their seats in this body."[8] In this manner, the Democrats came into control of the House. The House then adjourned until Saturday,

then until Monday, and then until Tuesday, awaiting the
arrival of the new members.

In the Council, Republican by one vote, "four or five
leading Republicans," Governor Giddings wrote to the Secretary of State, "joined hands with the democrats and in the
absence of a most respectable and honorable Senator they
removed him and replaced him with a democrat and thereby
changed the political character of the Council. . . ."[9] Thus,
the Council became Democratic, seven to six.

Governor Giddings determined to reseat the four Republican members from Taos and control the House. Under
extreme pressure, several members who had voted to admit
the Taos contestants, including the Republican speaker,
changed their views and were desirous of restoring the original Taos Republicans to their seats.

The governor entered the House on Tuesday, January
9, and took a seat next to the speaker. He said that his ap-
pearance was "to prevent a hand to hand fight as it was
declared to me every member was armed and at any moment
a fight might occur."[10]

The House Journal of January 9 reported:

> Mr. H. Russell stated to the House that Mr. Julian
> Montoya was armed, and asked the sergeant at arms be
> authorized to disarm him, and that the arm be placed upon
> the Speaker's Table until adjournment . . . motion was
> adopted . . . and Mr. J. Montoya was disarmed.

The Santa Fe *Weekly Post* editorially criticized Giddings' visit as a simple attempt at intimidation:

> In this instance he came not as an official of his stand-
> ing should come into the body of the House but to wait
> among the rabble and counsel revolutionary and disorgan-

izing proceeding and then screen the perpetrators under the cloak of his official dignity.[11]

With the governor present on Tuesday, January 9, Republican Speaker Milnor Rudulph took the floor and sought to amend Friday's Journal, which recorded the voting on the new representatives from Taos, by declaring the Journal null and void and asking to destroy its contents. His motion failed by a vote of 10 to 11. The House then adjourned until Wednesday, January 10.

Later, House Speaker Rudulph wrote to Secretary of State Hamilton Fish, on February 24, 1872:

> I immediately set about consulting with my friends as to the most effectual practicable means to reinstate those injured parties, and by advice of Gov. Giddings, the Hons. Joseph G. Palen and H. S. Johnson of the Supreme Court, and several other lawyers of Santa Fe, I determined at the first practicable moment to declare the true members from Taos unjustly and illegally deprived of their seats, that act, of a consequence, null and void . . . and I, now, only waited a favorable opportunity for carrying out my plan.

Wednesday, January 10, 1872, the House gallery and passageways began filling early in the morning. The speaker later reported: " . . . it was with great difficulty I effected a passage through the dense crowd that already occupied the passageway and gallery, and to my great surprise, almost everyone whom I was obliged to move from my course, I found armed with a pistol. . . ."[12]

The House was called to order at twelve o'clock, and the roll was called. The speaker, fearing a mob had filled the gallery, rose and ordered the sergeant at arms to clear the gallery and entrance, and ordered all spectators to leave.

Representative Russell objected to the order, and appealed from the order of the speaker to the House. The speaker refused to recognize any motions as they came in great numbers from the opposition, insisting that his order to clear the gallery and the entrances be carried out. In his subsequent report, the speaker defended his action:

> This order was at once attacked by the whole force of the opposition . . . on my insisting upon my order being obeyed there were a number of appeals from my order, motions upon motions were crowded upon me, and as long as my order was not carried out, I declared all appeals and motions not in order. Several of the democrats called upon the mob in the gallery not to obey the sergeant at arms, but to remain where they were. I called upon the sheriff of Santa Fe county, whom I saw present to assist the sergeant at arms to carry out the order I had given him. He positively refused to do anything in the matter.

After about an hour of confusion, the speaker, without a motion from the floor, ordered the House adjourned. In his report, he explained:

> This state of things continued about an hour and seeing there was little or no possibility of commanding order, I arose and in a loud voice . . . informed them that I considered their actions scandalous in the extreme . . . I felt justified in bringing the session to a close. I therefore declared the House adjourned, and left the chair and the hall, accompanied by all the republican members, but in the passageway I was met by the Governor, to whom I reported what I had done. His Excellency did me the honor to approve all of my course in the matter but said it was a pity I had not adjourned the House to some fixed date and hour;

so I determined though I deemed it at a great deal of risk to myself . . . to remedy this error. . . . I immediately returned to the House . . . called the House to order and announced that the adjournment was to ten o'clock on the following day.[13]

The Democrats, left in the chamber, remained in their seats and immediately organized their House:

> The Hon. Branch was appointed temporary Speaker who then called the House to order, stating that the House had not adjourned, for the reason that the vote of the members had not been taken, and that the Speaker had no authority to adjourn the House without the consent therefor.[14]

The rules were then suspended, and Mr. Russell introduced the following resolution:

> "Whereas, Mr. Rudulph has abandoned his seat as Speaker of this House without the consent thereof; therefore, be it resolved that the position held by the said Rudulph in this House be declared vacant," which resolution was adopted; whereupon they chose J. R. Johnson as the new Speaker.[15]

The new speaker was authorized to "order the chief clerk to issue a writ directed to the sergeant at arms to bring before this House the absent members. . . ."

The new sergeant at arms, H. Clay Carson, attempting to arrest Milnor Rudulph, reported that he "entered the public office of His Excellency, Marsh Giddings . . . and was about to call a force to my assistance when His Excellency interfered, and said to me, 'don't you bring any person or persons into my office to arrest anyone.' I thereupon left the

Governor's office without making the arrest."[16] Later, however, the sergeant at arms gathered a posse and took Rudulph
by force to the House.

Late on January 10, Speaker Milnor Rudulph requested
of Col. Gordon Granger, commanding the United States
military district for New Mexico:

> [Let us have] a sufficient number of the soldiers under
> your command . . . stationed at the door of the Legisla-
> tive Assembly tomorrow morning early to prevent the en-
> trance into the said House or lobby of all persons not con-
> nected with the said Legislative Assembly . . . there is
> great danger that before the hour to which the adjournment
> of said House was made, the Hall of said House will be
> filled up, under the direction and by the procurment [sic] of
> certain evil disposed persons, with men who have no right to
> seats therein. . . .[17]

Governor Giddings endorsed the request: " . . . it is prudent to have a force of soldiers present as requested by the
Speaker . . . and therefore I request you to provide such
force at the time and for the purpose aforesaid as requested
by the Speaker."[18]

On January 11, under the protection of the United
States Army, Speaker Rudulph recognized his opportunity
to reseat the Taos Republicans. He entered the House and
found J. R. Johnson presiding—the Democrats had remained
in session all night in order to be in firm control the next
morning. Yet, when Rudulph demanded that Johnson vacate
the speaker's chair, he did so immediately. A roll call showed
that a quorum was present.

Speaker Rudulph then acted to reseat the Republican
members from Taos:

In view of the violent, unjust, deceptions and illegal
means employed for the expulsion of the true and lawful
members from Taos county, I could not but consider that
step null and void, I therefore, as Speaker of the House of
Representatives declare those gentlemen as fully entitled to
their seats in this body, and to all the rights and privileges as
members, as though they had never been deprived thereof,
and direct the Chief Clerk to call their names and none
other from Taos County.[19]

The Republican Taos members entered the chamber
and took their seats. This action met with such determined
and persistent opposition from the Democrats that Speaker
Rudulph began to think there would be a repetition of the
disorder of the previous day.[20]

The reseating of the Taos Republicans created two
Houses of Representatives. The Democrats left the regular
House and formed their own body, called the "Democrat
House." The regular body became the "Republican House."
The Republicans had a majority in their chamber by count-
ing the four Taos Republicans. Likewise, the Democrats had
a majority in their chamber by counting the four Taos
Democrats. Thus quorums were present in both Houses.

Speaker Rudulph reported: "From that time until the
adjournment of the legislature *sine die* these gentlemen were
not disturbed in the peaceful possession of their seats *nor did
the Democrats attend another session with us. . . .*"[21]

The Council report recorded the events:

Rudulph without having the journal read or allowing
a vote to be taken upon its approval or disapproval, declared . . . the original members from Taos, who had been

ousted as aforesaid, to take their seats as members of the
House. . . . This action led directly to a division of the
House of Representatives; and 11 members who remained
in the Hall on the 10th, together with the four Taos contestants above alluded to constitute one branch, with Mr.
John R. Johnson as Speaker, and the 11 members who left
the House on the 10th together with the original Taos
members, constituting the other branch, with Mr. Milnor
Rudulph, as Speaker.[22]

The Democrat House, on January 13, took possession
of the House Chamber by forcibly depriving the doorkeeper
of the keys to the chamber. On January 15, 1872, the Santa
Fe *New Mexican* protested: "Thus the House of Representatives of our Territory is deprived of the use of the hall
by violence . . . and is now without a suitable room in
which to meet. . . ."

Speaker Rudulph countered the occupation of the
chamber by a ruse of his own: " . . . during that night, by
the assistance of friends, I succeeded in removing the lock
from the door of the Hall and placed there another of a different key to that held by Johnson, so that, on the following
morning [January 16] he very unexpectedly discovered he
had been ousted of possession."[23]

The Council, controlled by the Democrats, 7 to 6, reprimanded Governor Giddings:

> In brief, the conduct of His Excellency and Mr.
> Rudulph throughout this entire controversy, seems to have
> been hasty, ill-considered, and highly discreditable to the
> official character of those gentlemen. . . . The action of
> His Excellency, Marsh Giddings, Gov. of said Territory
> . . . in making requisition for U.S. troops to be stationed
> in an about the halls of legislation . . . was hasty and ill-

considered in the extreme and entirely unwarranted by the
state of public feeling existing at the time such requisition
was made. . . .[24]

Both Houses met and passed measures during January.
Henry Wetter, secretary of the territory, telegraphed Secretary of State Fish on January 27:

> Time of Legislature expires February 1. Two bodies
> continue claiming to be House of Representatives. . . .
> Please instruct me as to which I shall pay. . . .[25]

On January 31, the Attorney General of the United
States refused to recognize either House as legal:

> I am satisfied that the papers placed in my hands,
> called a Journal, is an imperfect and one sided statement of
> what transpired between and including the 5th and the
> 10th instant and therefore it is unsafe basis for any opinion.
> . . . I think it quite probable that one division of the
> House has been acting altogether without a quorum and
> that the other division has been acting for at least a part
> of the time in the same way. . . . I do not consider it
> advisable to make any decision which may be construed into
> a recognition of either branch of the House as a legal
> body. . . .[26]

The division of the two Houses, however, was broken
January 29, two days before adjournment. The Council,
anxious for the passage of some laws, agreed to recognize
the Republican House if a new speaker were chosen. Governor Giddings approved measures only from the Republican House. The Supreme Court rendered a decision:

> The action of the House of Representatives on the
> fifth day of January A.D. 1872, whereby the [four Republi-

can] seats were declared vacant and four Democrats admitted to seats in the House of Representatives was unauthorized, illegal, revolutionary and void.[27]

Gregorio N. Otero, the new compromise speaker, replaced
Speakers Rudulph and Johnson.

Governor Giddings telegraphed Secretary Fish on
January 31:

> Original Rudulph House again working harmoniously
> with Council . . . Wetter refuses pay. Will you telegraph
> him to pay this House upon legal certificate of Speaker?[28]

The Legislature adjourned *sine die* at noon, February 1,
1872. Best remembered for the bitterness it created during
Governor Giddings' administration, this legislature accomplished much for New Mexico. The Santa Fe *New Mexican*
commented, editorially, March 22, 1872:

> The suggestions of the present Governor on the sub-
> jects of railroad, finance, taxation, the public debt, skilled
> labor, foreign capital, schools and education have in the
> main been regarded and acted upon. . . .

The compromise House, during the last two days of the
session, passed a revenue act placing a one percent ad
valorem tax on all property in the territory with one half of
the tax to be applied solely and exclusively for territorial
purposes and the remaining one half to be applied in like
manner for county and school purposes in the county
wherein the same is collected.

Nothing was done to improve the roads leading out of
the capital. The Santa Fe *Weekly New Mexican* reported,
June 24, 1873:

> There is not a road leading out of the city, that is pass-
> able or safe to travel on in the daylight let alone in the

darkness. Even horsemen, not to speak of vehicles, are in constant danger of running over some great "jump off." . . . The La Bajada road going south is absolutely unfit to travel. Passengers do not know at what moment the coach will upset and dash their brains out against the ragged rocks below. So great is the dread of this road, that the usual custom is to get out of the coach and walk down the frightful hills.

The 1872 legislature, acting as a constitutional convention, drafted, approved and submitted to the voters a state constitution. The purpose of the constitution was to help in successfully petitioning Congress for statehood. The voters of the territory approved the constitution June 3, 1872, but Congress refused to grant statehood.

The legislative revolt continued after the session with the rebels planning to remove Governor Giddings. Democrat Delegate to Congress Jose M. Gallegos wrote to President Grant March 13: "My people are extremely anxious to have Gov. Giddings removed as Governor; he's an offensive, meddling, disagreeable man to my people." Further, Gidding's son William, who served as librarian and adjutant general, was said to be a "man of bad habits, bad moral character." [29]

The President asked for an investigation.

In answering the charges, Giddings named his accusers and cited the reasons they desired to replace Judge Palen:

> Sullivan, a U.S. Officer [A. P. Sullivan, postmaster and editor of the Santa Fe *Post*] had been indicted for some criminal act under the charge of Judge Palen to which charge Sullivan took offense . . . Sec. Wetter [Henry Wetter, secretary of the territory] was charged with some wrong and I believe was also indicted by the grand jury. . . . Several wealthy parties in Santa Fe had become bound un-

der heavy bonds for the performance of certain duties. . . .
The causes were soon to be brought on for trial, and these
parties desired a more facile judge. Johnson [D. B. Johnson,
the judge in Mesilla who would have replaced Judge Palen]
had fallen into bad habits and appearances indicated to
these parties that they would be quite safe in his hands.
. . . Johnson is a drinking debauchee and is too low to be
respected by any. . . . Ex-Chief Justice Kirby Benedict
who is a bad man and has become very dissipated and has
been for a long time expelled from the courts for bad prac-
tices as a lawyer. . . . This John S. Watts was appointed
one of the District Judges for this Territory about 20 years
since. . . . Watts was never any lawyer except in name.
. . . These all combined to disgrace and get rid of Chief
Justice Palen.

It is mortifying to find myself called to account about
the habits and moral character of my appointees by a set
of men who have never [been] known to have any moral
character or political principles . . . and now that I have
accomplished so much that it seems a miracle.[30]

Giddings also told of something that had happened to
his thirty-year-old son, William M. Giddings:

. . . One night two [men] seized him right at my door.
I heard his voice and they pretended to arrest him. And he
thinking they had made a mistake which would disclose
itself when they reached the justice office where they pretended they were taking him walked on with them a little
until he began to suspect some wrong. When he resisted
and they coming to a dark place, one of them stepped back
and with a large stone struck him upon the head and felled
him to the ground and they followed up with repeated blows
until they thought him dead.[31]

Giddings' son recovered from the attack, and the charges against the governor and William were dismissed.

After the legislative revolt and the failure of the attempt to remove the governor, Marsh Giddings served New Mexico until the summer of 1875, and things went well for the territory. The year ending November 15, 1872, showed the effects of the new tax laws with collections of $49,429, and expenditures of only $41,711. When the next legislature met, in the winter of 1873, territorial warrants were at par value and the territorial indebtedness was small.

Governor Giddings addressed the legislature of 1873:

> Wisdom will direct a continuance of a policy dictated and sustained by law, which has been so quietly, pleasantly, and quickly inaugurated, by which the entire people shall through her schools become an enlightened people, and through her probity in meeting her financial engagements secure that character at home and abroad of which any people may be justly proud.[32]

Giddings suggested improving the school system by electing county and state superintendents. He recommended a reprint of the laws, equalization of tax assessments, encouragement of irrigation, inducement to immigrants to the territory, and clarification of private land grants. He cited facts and figures to demonstrate that New Mexico was ready for statehood.

Marsh Giddings was elated at the accomplishments of the two legislatures—accomplishments that could be ascribed, in part, to twenty years of trial and error in New Mexico. Some of the measures had been requested by previous governors, but during Giddings' administration, the need for such measures dawned upon the people and the legislature.

Governor Giddings remained a good Republican throughout his stay in New Mexico. He asserted that he helped draft the "first republican platform ever presented to the American people."[33]

He requested leave in the spring of 1872, to attend the National Convention as a delegate from the territory. In August he also requested leave, "so that I may go to the states to attend to some affairs of my own and incidentally may take part in the political campaign this fall."[34]

Beginning in January 1875, tragedy fell upon the governor and his family. He fell ill and by the first of February was confined to his bed. On February 27, his infant grandson, Harry Battles, son of his daughter, died at the Palace.

By the middle of March, Governor Giddings was too feeble to write. His secretary requested a sixty-day sick leave for the governor on March 24. It was granted and he planned to begin his absence when he was stronger.

He hoped to become strong enough to return to Michigan, but on May 31 he suffered a sudden relapse. By June 2 he had sold all his household furniture. An ambulance was loaded with the family baggage and while the ambulance was awaiting him at the door, he gradually sank into a state of unconsciousness which culminated in his death the following day, June 3, 1875, at the Palace of the Governors. The ambulance took the body East for burial.

Progress was made in New Mexico under Governor Giddings. Yet the unnoticed smouldering fires that would soon flame up in Lincoln County began in the closing days of his administration.

Dating back as far as February 3, 1874, there were rumblings in the territory, when the *Weekly New Mexican* reported, under the headline "The Lincoln County War":

A general distrust prevails throughout the whole section. Every man met is armed to the teeth. Up and down the Rio Hondo a number of ranchos have been deserted, and now many fine places could be purchased for a song, their owners and occupants being determined and anxious to depart from a place where the reign of peace and order will not apparently be reestablished, for a long time to come, and to where peace and quiet prevail now.

NOTES

1. Santa Fe *Weekly Post*, Sept. 2, 1871.

2. *Territorial Papers of the U.S. Department of State,* New Mexico, April 28, 1871—Nov. 16, 1872. National Archives, Washington.

3. Santa Fe *Weekly Post, loc. cit.*

4. *Territorial Papers of the U.S. Department of State, op. cit.*

5. Denver *Rocky Mountain News,* quoted in Santa Fe *Daily New Mexican,* Jan. 2, 1872.

6. *Territorial Papers of the U.S. Department of State, op. cit.,* "Report of the Committee of Investigation of the Council of the Legislative Assembly of the Territory of New Mexico Appointed to Examine into the Stationing of U.S. Troops in and about the Legislative Halls of Said Territory."

7. Santa Fe *Daily New Mexican,* Jan. 5, 1872.

8. *Territorial Papers of the U.S. Department of State, op. cit.*

9. *Ibid.*

10. *Ibid.*

11. Santa Fe *Weekly Post* quoted in Santa Fe *Daily New Mexican,* Jan. 11, 1872.

12. *Territorial Papers of the U.S. Department of State, op. cit.,* "Statement of Milnor Rudulph to Secretary of State Hamilton Fish."

13. *Ibid.*

14. *Ibid.*

15. *Territorial Papers of the U.S. Department of State, op. cit.*

16. *Ibid.*

17. *Ibid.*

18. *Ibid.*

19. *Territorial Papers of the U.S. Department of State, op. cit.,* "Statement of Milnor Rudulph."

20. *Ibid.*

21. *Ibid.*

22. *Territorial Papers of the U.S. Department of State, op. cit.,* "Report of the Committee of Investigation."

23. *Territorial Papers of the U.S. Department of State, op. cit.*, "Statement of Milnor Rudulph."

24. *Territorial Papers of the U.S. Department of State, op. cit.*, "Report of the Committee of Investigation."

25. *Territorial Papers of the U.S. Department of State, op. cit.*

26. *Ibid.*

27. *Ibid.*

28. *Ibid.*

29. *Selected Letters Received by the appointment Division and Miscellaneous Division, Concerning Gov. Marsh Giddings, 1873-75,* National Archives, Washington.

30. *Ibid.*

31. *Ibid.*

32. Santa Fe *Weekly New Mexican,* Dec. 9, 1873.

33. *Territorial Papers of the U.S. Department of State, op. cit.*

34. *Ibid.*

SAMUEL B. AXTELL

NINE

Corruption, Fraud, and Murder

SAMUEL B. AXTELL

1875-78

ITIZENS OF NEW MEXICO ANTICIPATED PROSPERITY
and the granting of statehood to the territory in July
1875, when Samuel B. Axtell became the new governor. The future was bright, especially since there was a
peaceful interval in the Indian trouble.

Governor Axtell reported to the legislature December
6, 1875: "We are at peace with the Indian tribes within our
Territory. . . . In the Southeast portion of the Territory
the earth has been kept moist with the blood of citizens . . .
[until] within the last four years not a murder has been committed by Indians."[1]

In that year, 1875, statehood for New Mexico almost
became a reality. Under the direction of Territorial Congressional Delegate Stephen B. Elkins, the measure passed
both houses of Congress for the first time, but because of
an unfortunate handshake, New Mexico failed to gain statehood.[2] However, in view of prevailing security, prosperity
and.stability, New Mexico citizens were confident the prize
was within reach.

Yet, within the three years of Governor Axtell's administration, New Mexico was torn by civil war in several parts

of the territory. Conditions became so desperate that a special agent for the United States Department of Interior, Frank Warner Angel, stated in his official report: "It is seldom that history states more corruption, fraud, mismanagement, plots and murders, than New Mexico has been the theatre [of] under the administration of Governor Axtel [sic]." Angel's report was to substantiate a charge that the governor "conspired to murder innocent and law abiding citizens because they opposed his wishes and were exerting their influence against him."[3]

Samuel B. Axtell became New Mexico's chief executive July 30, 1875, after serving in various political positions in other parts of the country. He was born in Columbus, Ohio, on October 14, 1819. He attended local schools and graduated from Western Reserve College, Hudson, Ohio. He studied law, was admitted to the bar in 1842, and practiced law in Michigan until 1851. In that year, he moved to California to engage in the mining business. He helped establish Amador County and was district attorney of the new county for six years. In 1860, he opened a law office in San Francisco. Axtell was elected as a Democrat to Congress from the First Congressional District of California in 1866. He was reelected two years later. He was not a candidate for election in 1870.[4]

Axtell changed his party affiliation and became a Republican during the administration of Ulysses S. Grant. President Grant then appointed Axtell governor of Utah, an office he held from February 2, 1875, until the middle of June 1875.

While governor of Utah, Axtell was accused of being too sympathetic to the Mormons. By signing a certificate of election to a Mormon Congressional delegate, he found himself in a Mormon—anti-Mormon factional fight. Axtell went

quietly to Washington and obtained for himself an appointment as governor of New Mexico.

The transfer from Utah to New Mexico was accomplished in a brief communication, June 5, 1875, from President Grant to the Department of Interior: "Offer Axtell
Governorship New Mexico and appoint Emery in his place
if he accepts. Emery may be appointed to New Mexico otherwise."[5]

Axtell arrived in Santa Fe on July 30, 1875, and at once
took up his official duties. In his first address to the territorial legislature on December 6, 1875, Governor Axtell called
for small reforms to improve the government of New Mexico. He asked "revision and reprint of the laws." He said
there existed "a tendency . . . to over legislate. The world
is not only governed too much, but it has too many laws."

He suggested Sunday closings, holding territorial elec-
tions on the same date as the presidential election, and proposed a territorial prison. He called for the education of
both sexes and asked for women teachers. He requested an
appropriation for roads in the territory, and also an appropriation for preserving the archives.

Events that were to counter the fine beginning of Governor Axtell's administration were taking place in the territory, particularly in Colfax and Lincoln counties. Two
acts of the 1876 territorial legislature and two murders
would soon explode into civil conflict.[6]

A Methodist minister, F. J. Tolby, was murdered on
September 14, 1875, in a lonely canyon between Elizabethtown and Cimarron in Colfax County. Two and a half years
later, February 18, 1878, John H. Tunstall was murdered
in Lincoln County. These two events were unrelated, except
that each led Samuel B. Axtell into difficulties.

Leading citizens of Colfax County found that two legislative acts of 1876 affected them adversely. One measure authorized the courts to partition or place for sale land grants, even if petitioned by a small owner. The effect of this measure was to jeopardize large land holdings and make it possible for any party at interest to force partition and sale.

The second act, passed January 14, 1876, annexed Colfax County to Taos County for all judicial purposes for a minimum of two terms of court. The effect of the two acts together was to give Taos courts jurisdiction over court cases involving land grants in Colfax County. The citizens of Colfax learned of the court measure only after it had passed the legislature. They hastily telegraphed the governor, asking for a hearing before he acted upon the measure. The governor replied with a telegram that read only: "BILL SIGNED. S. B. AXTELL."[7] Whatever he intended by the message, Axtell was not forgiven for refusing to hear the citizens of Colfax County before acting on the measure.

The citizens of Colfax County held a mass meeting, November 10, 1875, which was reported in the Cimarron *News and Press.* The purpose of the meeting was to consider the facts connected with the murder of the Rev. F. J. Tolby. A resolution of the meeting charged:

> The facts disclosed reveal deliberately planned assassination in which the men Cruz Vega [previously lynched by a mob] and Manuel Cardenas [shot to death when being returned to jail] were the tools of other parties who from some motive, aside from plunder, planned the murder and procured the two men above named to perform the cowardly act.

The resolution was signed by the Rev. O. P. McMains (later tried for murder in the lynching of Cruz Vega) as chairman, and Frank Springer, as secretary.

At the meeting it was stated that Tolby was murdered for attempting to interfere with the influence of a group of leading Santa Fe citizens, called "The Ring," in controlling Colfax County. Governor Axtell was accused of supporting members of "The Ring." A meeting, held in Santa Fe on November 26, 1875, and reported in the New York *Sun,* December 22, 1875, issued a statement which said, in part:

> . . . the actual murderers were hunted down and when it was found that they implicated the principal members of the Colfax County branch of the "Ring" as instigators of the crime, the indignation of the people knew no bound. At one time it was feared that every one of the politicians named in connection with the murder would be strung up by the neck without the intervention of judge or jury. . . .

Frank Springer, reporting under oath his conversation with Governor Axtell in February 1876, concerning the attaching of Colfax to Taos County for judicial purposes, asked Axtell to visit Colfax County. Springer said:

> In response, the Governor absolutely refused to visit Colfax County . . . until the people showed a different disposition. Said Axtell was, during this conversation, very bitter in his allusion to the people of Colfax County. . . .[8]

On October 30, 1875, Cruz Vega was lynched by a mob which suspected him of killing Reverend Tolby. The Rev. O. P. McMains was held for instigating the lynching party and was tried for murder. His bond was set at $15,000. A local correspondent, writing for the Pueblo, Colorado, *Chieftain,* April 27, 1877, defended McMains, implying that he was being persecuted for standing up for the murdered Tolby:

Mr. McMains had nothing whatever to do with the lynching of the murder[er]s of Tolby. . . . This plan of bringing suits against men obnoxious to the ring is an old dodge. . . . People here are in constant fear and nobody dares to raise his voice against the terrible anarchy we are undergoing in this county. These gentlemen . . . seem to have an absolute power in everything in New Mexico. They run our legislature and make this ignorant people pass such laws as will gratify their rapacious ambition. They control the courts to such an extent that respectable citizens regard them as a public calamity. The lawyers of New Mexico with the exception of a very few honorable exceptions, are members of this corrupt Ring.

Charges leveled against Axtell were sent to Secretary of the Interior Carl Schurz and to the President in April 1877. The first charge criticized the governor:

[He allowed] the removal of the said court from Cimarron, Colfax county, on about March 1876, to Taos, Taos county, a distance of about 50 miles for the purpose, it is alleged of punishing the people of Colfax county for attempting to ferret out the perpetrators of a cold-blooded murder of a Methodist preacher, named Tolby, which the officers of the law had failed and declined to do.[9]

Another charge accused Axtell of collusion with "The Ring." Its members were said to be attempting to break up the land grants for their own benefit and to induce Mormon settlement. There was a good deal of anti-Mormon sentiment in New Mexico after the Civil War. And Axtell had been accused of being a Mormon after he published some letters in the Salt Lake City *Herald* over the Spanish signature, *El Obispo,* which translates as "The Bishop." In connection with this accusation, Brigham Young wrote to the Secretary of Interior on July 13, 1877: "The statement that he [Axtell] is a Bishop in the Church of Jesus Christ of Latter Day Saints, or that he has been baptized into the Church is entirely without foundation in Truth."[10]

Another of the charges sent to the Secretary of Interior alleged:

> [The legislature] under the dictation of this Ring of speculators, recently passed a law, by which the district court can order the whole of a grant to be sold at public auction, upon such notice as it sees fit, upon the demand of any one of the parties in interest no matter how small that interest may be. By this means all these grants are to be forced to sale, for cash and as the titles are in an unsettled state, and most of the papers and records are in the hands of the Ring, there can be little competition in bidding.[11]

Axtell answered the charges May 30, 1877, in a letter to the Secretary of Interior:

> . . . As to legislation in Colfax county, I am in full accord with the Territorial legislature, the Chief Justice, United States Attorney General, and other good men. We believe we are acting for the best. I have no interest to act otherwise than for the public good. The bill was passed by nearly a unanimous vote in the Legislature and for the sole purpose of bringing to justice certain parties who seemed to overawe the juries in that county. Colfax was formerly a part of Taos. . . .[12]

On June 14, Governor Axtell addressed another letter to Secretary of Interior Carl Schurz:

> I am not a convert to the Mormon faith. . . . It is true that I wrote some letters to the Salt Lake Herald over the signature of "El Obispo". . . . My letters . . . had no religious, political, or business significance. . . . Second, it is absolutely untrue that I have connected myself with a

corrupt combination of men, forming a powerful "ring" to procure legislation. . . . I did not assist to procure the passage of a law entitled "An Act Relating to the Partition of Real Estate and for Other Purposes". I signed the bill as passed by the legislature but I deny that it has or was intended to have the effect stated in the charges. . . . I deny that I with the combination of men referred to secured the enactment of laws especially inimical to the people of Colfax County. . . .

I was and still am satisfied that the annexation of Colfax county was intended not to obstruct justice as charged but to secure the just enforcement of the laws.[13]

Governor Axtell expressed concern about the murder of Tolby, stating that he did not know Tolby, that the murder was committed shortly after his arrival, that he had quickly offered a $500 reward for the arrest of the murderer, and that he had no reason to believe that any "Ring" or persons at Santa Fe had any connection with the murder.

Friends of Axtell rallied, and flooded Washington with petitions and statements in his behalf. A typical petition was sent from San Miguel County in July 1877: "We the undersigned citizens of New Mexico desire to express to you our appreciation of the general administration of his Excellency, S. B. Axtell, as Governor of New Mexico and protest against his removal."

The petition from Santa Fe was signed "by the best citizens of this city irrespective of politics." Friends from Doña Ana County petitioned the President, "expressing our entire confidence in the capacity and integrity of Gov. Axtell. . . ." The citizens favoring Governor Axtell included William G. Ritch, secretary of the territory; S. B. Elkins, former congressional delegate from New Mexico; William

Breeden, attorney general of New Mexico, and New Mexico congressional delegate J. Romero.[14]

When the twenty-third legislature convened January 7, 1878, Governor Axtell could not have anticipated the explosion that would soon take place in New Mexico. Addressing the legislature on January 7, the governor expressed optimism:

> The general condition of the Territory is far more prosperous and promising now than it has ever been before. Railroads are rapidly approaching us from the North and the West; the telegraphic wire has been extended the entire length of the Territory. . . . Improved wagon roads have given us cheaper freights and quicker communication with our neighbors. . . . Our mines have yielded good returns for the labor expended by our citizens. . . .

His comments on law enforcement gave the only indication of impending trouble:

> Besides bad Indians, we have bad white men, who need the strong hand of government to restrain them from preying upon their fellow men. I will cite a recent instance in Lincoln County, for the purpose of stimulating you to memorialize Congress to permit the regular army to aid the civil authorities of New Mexico to preserve the public peace. Four desperate men, outlaws and robbers, were roaming over Lincoln county; the sheriff raised a posse of some thirty men, surrounded their camp and made them prisoners. He brought them to Lincoln . . . and confined them in such a jail as a new county in a new country is able to have. . . . The confederates of the prisoners collected in the vicinity . . . some 30 men, and gave out publicity that they intended to rescue them. . . . The rescue was made and these desperadoes were set at liberty. . . .[15]

Less than three weeks after the legislature adjourned on February 15, 1878, Governor Axtell was forced to telegraph the President of the United States, March 3, 1878: "I am unable to enforce the law and to protect life and property in this Territory and request assistance from the President."[16]

The citizens of Colfax County still did not like Axtell and continued to speculate on how they might effect his removal. Meanwhile, the feuding in Lincoln County exploded three days after the close of the legislature with the killing of a young Englishman, John H. Tunstall.

The Lincoln County War, as it was called, involved all the elements of lawlessness in the territory. The conflict was between newcomers and residents of long standing, between cattle ranchers and cattle thieves, between established businesses and new enterprises, between rival gangs of murderers and outlaws. The residents of long standing had the officers of the law and the governor on their side.

Lawrence G. Murphy, leading Lincoln County citizen, controlled the business of the county. He came to New Mexico in military service and remained, and so qualified as an old resident. He took James J. Dolan and John H. Riley as partners. The business group became friendly with all the officials of the territory, including Governor Axtell. They were on such good terms that Mr. Riley, in May 1876, loaned Governor Axtell $1800. The local sheriff, district attorney, and even the United States district attorney, were very friendly with Murphy, Dolan and Riley.

Attorney Alexander A. McSween, arriving in Lincoln in 1875, at first did legal work for Murphy and his associates, but he soon became friendly with others interested in business—John S. Chisum, sometimes referred to as "the Cattle

King," R. D. Hunter of St. Louis, and the Englishman, John
H. Tunstall. In the fall of 1877, McSween and Tunstall were
ready to open a mercantile business in Lincoln in competition with Dolan and Riley. The Murphy partners were not
willing to accept competition in an area which they controlled. Each group attempted to spoil the plans of the other.
McSween was charged with embezzlement of the proceeds
of an insurance policy belonging to one of his clients. Judge
Warren Bristol authorized the issuance of a warrant for Mc-
Sween's arrest.

John Chisum was arrested along with McSween, on
December 27, 1877. From jail, Chisum protested to Governor Axtell, but without result. On January 18, 1878, Tunstall countered the arrest of his partner, McSween, by writing a letter to the Mesilla *Independent,* published January
26, in which he alleged that Sheriff William Brady had ma-
nipulated Lincoln County tax collections for the use and
benefit of Dolan and Riley:

> Alex A. McSween Esq., of this place paid him (Sheriff
> Brady) over fifteen hundred dollars by cheque on the First
> National Bank of Santa Fe. . . . Said cheque was presented
> for payment by John H. Riley Esq., of the firm of J. J.
> Dolan and Co., this last amount was paid by the last named
> gentleman to Underwood and Nash for cattle. Thus passed
> away over fifteen hundred dollars belonging to the Terri-
> tory of New Mexico.

Dolan replied that Brady's tax accounts were perfectly
regular. But the Sheriff, Dolan, and Riley were further em-
bittered against the rival business group. As matters turned
out, by publishing the letter young John Tunstall seemed to
have sentenced himself to death.

There was additional legal skirmishing between the two factions. Then District Attorney William L. Rynerson, February 14, 1878, wrote to Riley and Dolan:

> I believe Tunstall is in with the swindles with the rogue McSween. . . . I will aid to punish the scoundrels all I can. . . . Have good men about to aid Brady and be assured I shall help you all I can . . . for I believe there was never found a more scoundrely set than that outfit.[17]

The sheriff, encouraged by the letter from the district attorney, decided to attach McSween's property to satisfy any possible claims arising from the insurance suit. The sheriff attached all of the merchandise in the Tunstall store and the home of McSween. Then the sheriff's posse rode out to attach McSween's interest in Tunstall's ranch. On February 18, 1878, while he was riding back to Lincoln, several members of the posse waylaid Tunstall and killed him. This opened the conflict and began the bloody Lincoln County War.

Justice of the Peace John B. Wilson conducted an inquest in the village of Lincoln. The verdict read:

> [Tunstall] came to his death on 18 Feb., 1878, by means of divers bullets shot and sent forth out of and from deadly weapons . . . which said deadly weapons then and there were held by . . . Jesse Evans, Frank Baker, Thomas Hill, George Hindman, J. J. Dolan, William Morton. . . .[18]

Sheriff Brady wrote to District Attorney Rynerson on March 4, and to U.S. District Attorney T. B. Catron, to justify the action of his posse. He said: "Anarchy is the only word which would truthfully describe the situation here for the past month. . . ."[19]

T. B. Catron referred the letter to Governor Axtell, who telegraphed a summary to Washington asking the President to allow federal troops to assist territorial officers in serving legal processes and maintaining public peace. Governor Axtell then left for Lincoln.

Axtell issued a proclamation on March 9, 1878, which showed both factions that he stood squarely on the side of the Murphy partners. His proclamation relieved Justice of the Peace John B. Wilson and U.S. Marshal Robert Widenmann of their official duties. Axtell stated that John B. Wilson's appointment by the county commissioners as a justice of the peace was illegal and void. This ruling was difficult to understand, for Governor Axtell had signed, on January 13, 1876, a measure authorizing county commissioners to appoint justices of the peace to fill vacancies. Axtell's proclamation continued: "It follows from the above statements that there is no legal process in this case to be enforced, except the writs and processes issued out of the Third Judicial District Court by Judge Bristol and there are no Territorial civil officers here to enforce these except Sheriff Brady and his deputies. . . ."[20]

On the date of the proclamation, Frank Baker and William Morton, members of the posse which killed Tunstall, were killed, apparently in reprisal for the Englishman's death.

The following week, on March 16, 1878, Montague R. Leverson, a new Lincoln County resident, wrote to the President about conditions in Lincoln County and asked for the removal of Governor Axtell:

> The murder of Tunstall was plotted and contrived by the District Attorney of the third judicial district by whom the District Judge is used as a tool. I deeply regret to add that the Governor has illegally and despotically exerted his power to screen the murderers. . . . I think it probable that the conduct of the Governor has been influenced more by weakness and want of intelligence than intentional

criminality, but the consequences are equally pernicious as though it had been influenced by the latter.[21]

Leverson concluded by asking for the suspension of Axtell.

The answer to Governor Axtell's proclamation of March 9, 1878, was the killing of Sheriff Brady and a deputy sheriff in broad daylight on the street of Lincoln, April 1, 1878, by members of the McSween faction. Among those accused of killing the sheriff was William Bonney, known as "Billy the Kid."

On April 26, a letter was addressed to President Rutherford B. Hayes on stationery of McSween and Shield, law offices, Lincoln County Bank Building: "The undersigned have the honor of transmitting to you . . . a copy of the proceedings of a meeting held by the citizens of Lincoln County, New Mexico, relating to the late trouble."[22] The public meeting, held on April 24, at which B. H. Ellis and A. A. McSween both were elected secretaries, issued the following statement:

> That we condemn without qualification the conduct of the Governor S. B. Axtell while here in March last. That his refusal to investigate our troubles stamps him as a little one-sided partisan. That his conduct and proclamation of March 9, 1878, are unworthy of an officer filling his exalted station. That as a result of that proclamation he is responsible for the loss of life that has occurred in this county since his visit. . . .

One resolution clearly foreshadowed future events:

> That we recognize our mutual dependence upon each other and that we pledge our lives and our property to the protection of each other. . . . That we tender our thanks to John S. Copeland for having accepted the office of sheriff

and for his important and efficient discharge of duty as
such since he took charge.[23]

The public meeting of April 24 which praised Sheriff
John S. Copeland was unpalatable to Dolan and Riley. They
complained to Axtell who removed Copeland and replaced
him with George W. Peppin. The Governor said in his
letter to Copeland: " . . . you have failed to file your bond
as collector of taxes . . . more than thirty days have elapsed
since you have been acting as Sheriff, [so] it becomes my
duty to remove you from office. . . ."[24]

A grand jury met in Lincoln County in April 1878, and,
although Judge Warren Bristol attempted to persuade the
jury against A. A. McSween, the jury asserted its independence, criticizing the governor and the anti-McSween faction:

> The grand jury for the April 1878 term of the District
> Court of Lincoln County, deeply deplore the present in-
> security of life and property. . . . Had his excellency, S. B.
> Axtell when here, ascertained from the people the cause of
> our troubles, as he was requested, valuable lives would have
> been spared our community; especially do we condemn that
> portion of his proclamation relating to J. B. Wilson as J. P.
> Mr. Wilson acted in good faith as such J. P. for over a year.
> . . . We believe that had the governor done his duty while
> here, these unfortunate occurrences would have been
> spared us.[25]

The grand jury indicted John Middleton, Hendry Brown
and William Bonney—all McSween men—for the murder
of Sheriff William Brady.

During the latter part of June and the early part of
July, both factions—Dolan, Riley and partisans on one side
and the McSween faction on the other—prepared for the
showdown that appeared inevitable. The Las Vegas *Gazette*

of June 22 commented: "Reports from Lincoln county indicate a renewal of hostilities between adverse factions; both parties are in the field and a collision is imminent."

Sheriff Peppin sent riders throughout the territory, promising deputy sheriffs' commissions to all who would augment his party. Gunfighters came to Lincoln from Doña Ana County and elsewhere. McSween, after visiting John S. Chisum, brought forty-one men back to Lincoln with him. McSween and his group established themselves in the McSween home at the edge of the village.

The final episode began July 16, when shots were fired in Lincoln. That day, a stray bullet grazed a soldier from Fort Stanton. For that reason, sixty cavalrymen entered Lincoln and a warrant was issued for the arrest of McSween and others of his group for attempted murder of the soldier.

Even though he knew of the crisis in Lincoln county, the governor telegraphed Secretary Schurz July 17, 1878, requesting a ninety-day leave.

July 19, 1878, climaxed the fighting which had continued sporadically since July 16. It was a day the public meeting had anticipated in the statement of April 26 to President Hayes: "We pledge our lives and our property to the protection of each other."

On this day, William Bonney became for all time "Billy the Kid," and a bloody chapter was written in New Mexico history.

Sheriff Peppin planned to serve the warrant on McSween for wounding the soldier. He was aware that he would be protected under the law for killing anyone in the party who resisted or who appeared to do so. Toward dusk, July 19, after shots were exchanged between the factions all day, the McSween home was set afire. McSween and his followers were called upon to surrender, but they began shooting. In the firing, McSween and three of his followers were killed, and one of Peppin's men died. William Bonney escaped under heavy fire from the sheriff's men. Four men lay dead. Nothing had been resolved. The death of McSween deprived that faction of leadership. Many court actions and several deaths were to follow, but after the climactic three-day battle the trouble began to abate.

In addition to the complete breakdown of law and order in Lincoln County, Governor Axtell found himself in new trouble in Colfax County. In the spring of 1878, Frank Springer of Cimarron had come into possession of a letter written by Axtell two years earlier. The letter appeared to refer to a plan to assassinate Springer. In March of 1876, Springer and twelve or fifteen others had invited the governor to visit Colfax County.

Springer wrote to the Secretary of Interior about the matter and enclosed a copy of Axtell's letter of 1876, addressed to Benjamin Stevens, territorial district attorney. This letter had fallen into Springer's hands only two months before. The letter from Axtell to Stevens read:

DEAR BEN:

The second telegram delivered to you at Fort Union directed to Cimarron was intended to leak, but the operator here says he cannot raise the Cimarron office. If I was expected our friends would probably be on hand, as the guard is only a Government escort. I do not think your definite business is suspected. Wade informed Hatch that he had been ready all the time to assist you, but could not find that you wanted to do it. Hatch says their opinion is that you weakened and do not want to arrest the man [R. C. Allison]. Have your men placed to arrest him and to kill all the men who resist you or stand with those who do resist you. Our man signed the invitation with others who were at that meeting, for me to visit Colfax—Porter, Morely, Springer, et al. Now, if they expect me Saturday, they will be on hand. Send me letters by messenger, and do not hesitate at extreme measures. Your honor is at stake now, and a failure is fatal. If others resist or attempt murder bring them also. Hatch is excited and wishes, of course, to put all the blame on the civil officers. I am more anxious on your account than for any other reason. I clearly see that we have no friends in Colfax, and I have suspected all along that some of our pretended friends here were traitors. Yours,　S. B. AxTELL.

When Frank Springer obtained the letter, he directed a letter to Governor Axtell, demanding the governor's reason for seeking his death. Axtell replied, "There is some very grave mistake in the whole matter. I am not an assassin, never desired the death of any human being."[27] Springer again wrote Axtell, asking him to explain wherein the "very grave mistake" consisted. Axtell replied: "I regret that any ambiguity in my letter should have led you to believe that violence was intended toward yourself or any other peaceful citizen."[28]

The Cimarron *News and Press* on April 18, 1878, reported the entire story under the heading, "A Page of History—Dedicated to S. B. Axtell." The story read: " . . . upon that extraordinary epistle we forbear extended comment at present. It may be, like the celebrated 'El Obispo' letter, only a joke—a ghastly joke!" On May 23, the *News and Press* printed another story:

> Five weeks ago we published the above letter and telegram together with a succinct account of the events of March 1876 . . . we have waited to hear what explanation [would be offered] . . . we did not expect any, as there is no way that we can see by which the infernal scheme disclosed in

this letter can be explained away. . . . By taking a fraudu-
lent and treacherous advantage of a courteous invitation,
he saw a chance to get a number of leading citizens of Colfax county into a trap in which there was a strong prob-
ability that a number of them would be killed. He knew
that such an event would bring about violence and disorder, and he doubtless also saw that on the turbulent wave,
with the assistance of United States forces, his exiled friends
could ride into power again. . . . Now we will leave it to
any fair man to say whether he can construe the above letter
into anything short of a plot to get some good men killed
. . . by the Governor of New Mexico. By the representative of the power, majesty, and dignity of the United States.
. . . In what age, and what country do we live, that such
iniquity and disgrace should be enthroned among us?

Frank Springer and Governor Axtell also differed
sharply over the removal of the sheriff of Colfax County.
Mr. Springer charged that the governor removed the sheriff
to replace him with a person of the governor's choice. The
governor denied this, saying that the sheriff had resigned:
"Mr. Springer makes another mistake and swears to it. He
says I removed the Sheriff of Colfax county. The Sheriff
resigned, and Mr. Springer knows it."[29]

However, Axtell's removal order which substantiated
Springer's allegation, was printed in the *News and Press,*
September 28, 1878: " It appearing to me by the certificate
of the clerk of the District Court, 1st Judicial District that
you have failed to file your bond as required by law you
are therefore removed from the office of Sheriff of Colfax
county. Respectfully yours, S. B. AXTELL."

Time was running out for Axtell as chief executive of
New Mexico. During the middle of May, 1878, the Department of Interior and the Department of Justice sent Frank

Warner Angel, New York attorney, to New Mexico as a special agent to examine the situation. Angel's official report began:

> Under your instructions I visited New Mexico for the purpose of ascertaining if there was any truth in the repeated complaints made to the Department as to fraud, incompetency, and corruption of United States officials. . . . I was met by every opposition possible by the United States civil officials and every obstacle thrown in my way by them to prevent a full and complete examination . . . the following charges in substance were made against the Governor of said Territory.

Then Angel listed six charges pertaining to affairs in Lincoln County, three pertaining to Colfax County, and three general charges. Of the Lincoln County charges, he wrote:

> . . . I found Lincoln county convulsed by an internal war. I enquired the cause. Some one was responsible for the blood shed in that County. I found two parties in the field, one headed by Murphy Dolan and Riley—the other lead [sic] by McSween—both had done many things contrary to law. . . . The Governor came [and] heard the Murphy Dolan and Riley side, refused to hear the people who were with McSween or the residents of the county and acted strictly in advancing the Murphy Dolan and Riley party— Murder and unlawful acts followed instead of peace and quiet, which could have been accomplished if the Governor had acted as he should have done and listened patiently to both sides. The opportunity presented itself to him to have quieted and stopped the trouble in Lincoln county—by his partizan action he allowed it to pass and the continuations of the troubles that exist today in Lincoln county are

chargeable to him. He was a partizan either through corruption or weakness. . . .

Angel was critical of the removal of Justice of the Peace Wilson and Sheriff John Copeland in Lincoln County, but the
most serious charge concerned Colfax County. Of this, he
wrote: "[It is charged] that he conspired to murder innocent
and law abiding citizens because they opposed his wishes
and were exerting their influence against him."

Mr. Angel noted the background of the problem—the
division of Colfax County for judicial purposes, the refusal
of the governor to meet with a Colfax County delegation to
discuss the division, the bitterness of the governor toward
Colfax County, and the invitation of Colfax citizens for the
governor to meet with twelve or fifteen leaders.

Investigator Angel described a telegram Stevens received from the governor. Angel wrote:

> [Stevens] circulates the report that he is going to try
> and have the Governor visit Colfax . . . and exhibits a
> telegram from the Governor which reads as follows 'Do not
> let it be known that I will be in Cimarron on Saturday's
> coach . . .' and said it was proof that the Governor was
> coming to visit the County and would expect to meet those
> who had signed the invitation. . . . He requested that the
> matter be kept quiet as the Governor did not want a crowd
> but only wanted to meet those who had invited him. . . .
>
> The facts subsequently show that the Governor did
> not intend to visit Colfax county and that the action of
> Stevens was in furtherance of a plot as will appear by the
> following letter.

Angel quoted the "Dear Ben" letter in full, underlining the
sentence, *"have your men placed to arrest him* [R. C. Alli-

son] *and to kill all the men who resist you or stand with those who do resist you."* Angel's report continues:

> Was there ever a cooler devised plot with a Governor as sponsor? The Governor admits the letter. . . . He makes no attempt as to the telegram . . . by a downright falsehood he attempts to assemble certain persons who are obnoxious to him so that in the event of the resistance, to be arrested, of a person by the name of Allison an excuse would be offered 'to kill all the men who resist or stand with those who resist you.' He does not explain this; he cannot. . . . Any man capable of framing and trying to enforce such a letter of instructions as the one set forth in this report is not fit to be entrusted with any power whatever—I therefore report that this charge has been sustained. . . .
>
> It is seldom that history states more corruption, fraud, mismanagement, plots and murders, than New Mexico has been the theatre [of] under the administration of Governor Axtel [sic].[30]

Governor Axtell wrote to the President on September 9, 1878: "I beg respectfully to refer your Excellency to the above resolution [a church resolution favoring Governor Axtell] and to express the hope that I may be spared the mortification of removal when so near the close of my official term."[31]

Mr. Angel's report had been presented to the President in mid-August, and on September 4, Secretary of Interior Carl Schurz suspended S. B. Axtell and appointed Lew Wallace as his successor.

Lew Wallace arrived in Santa Fe September 29, and the following day took the oath of office. He immediately sent Axtell a note informing him that he, Wallace, had qualified, enclosing a copy of the order suspending Axtell. To save Axtell public embarrassment, Wallace requested that there be no public ceremony at his inauguration.

But ex-governor Axtell was not finished with New Mexico. He was able, as he had always been, to muster influential friends. On March 23, 1881, S. B. Elkins, former U.S. Attorney and congressional delegate, and law partner of Thomas B. Catron, asked the President to reappoint Axtell governor of New Mexico. Elkin's effort failed. However, on August 1, 1882, President Chester A. Arthur appointed Axtell chief justice of the territorial supreme court. He held this position until May 11, 1885, when his resignation was accepted by Grover Cleveland, the new President.

One of the events that occurred while Axtell was chief justice was the dispute over ownership of the Cañon del Agua mine in Santa Fe County. Young Miguel A. Otero, later governor, his brother Page B. Otero, attorney William A. Vincent, and others, were enjoined by Judge Axtell from entering upon the premises while the litigation was pending in the court. This action brought about a situation which Miguel Otero later recalled:

> As we declined to do this we were kept in the common jail of Santa Fe county, located on Water street, for a period of seven weeks. . . . Fortunately for us, Grover Cleveland was elected President and S. B. Axtell was removed. One of my attorneys, William A. Vincent, was appointed as Chief Justice to succeed him. . . . [Vincent was] my roommate in the Santa Fe county jail for seven long weeks.[32]

After his retirement from the supreme court, Axtell ran for probate judge of Santa Fe County, but lost by 600 votes. He died while visiting relatives in Morristown, Morris County, New Jersey, several years later.

When removed as governor by the President in 1878, Samuel B. Axtell left New Mexico to his successor in the most unsettled condition that had existed in territorial history.

NOTES

1. *Territorial Papers of the U.S. Department of Interior,* New Mexico, 1851-1914, Executive Proceedings, Oct. 8, 1874—Dec. 21, 1888.

2. In 1875, Stephen B. Elkins was Congressional delegate from New Mexico. On the basis of an eloquent speech by Elkins, a measure granting statehood to New Mexico passed the House by a vote of 160-54. In Elkins' speech, he claimed 130,000 population for New Mexico, although the 1870 census had counted only 91,000. He stressed the small public debt and the great natural resources of the territory, and recalled many earlier promises of statehood—from Stephen Watts Kearny, in the treaty of Guadalupe Hidalgo, and even by Gov. James S. Calhoun.

On Feb. 24, 1875, the measure passed the Senate by a decisive vote of 32-11, but with a slight amendment. It then had to return to the House for acceptance of the Senate change. Statehood for New Mexico seemed assured.

However, Elkins entered the House chamber one day just after Rep. Julius C. Burroughs of Michigan had ended a speech criticizing the South and the late rebellion. Elkins had not heard the speech, but he noticed a group around Burroughs, joined the crowd and shook Burroughs' hand. This action angered southerners who turned against Elkins and voted down the bill to grant statehood to New Mexico.

3. U.S. Department of Interior, *In the Matter of the Investigation of the Charges against S. B. Axtell, Governor of New Mexico,* dated Washington, Oct. 3, 1878, Frank Warner Angel, Special Agent, Dept. Interior.

4. *Biographical Directory of the American Congress, 1774-1949,* The Continental Congress and the Congress of the United States, Washington, Government Printing Office, 1950.

5. *Territorial Papers of the U.S. Department of Interior, op. cit.*

6. *Ibid.*

7. *Ibid.*

8. *Ibid.*

9. *Ibid.*

10. *Ibid.*

11. *Ibid.*

12. *Ibid.*

13. *Ibid.*

14. Record of the Office of the Secretary of the Interior, Appointments Division: *Selected Documents pertaining to S. B. Axtell and Lew Wallace, Governors of the Territory* of New Mexico, 1875-1882, National Archives, Washington.

15. *Territorial Papers of the U.S. Department of Interior, op. cit.*

16. *Ibid.*

17. William A. Keleher, *Violence in Lincoln County, 1869-1881, A New Mexico Item,* Albuquerque, Univ. of New Mexico Press, 1957.

18. Warren A. Beck, *New Mexico, A History of Four Centuries,* Norman, Univ. of Oklahoma Press, 1962.

19. Keleher, *op. cit.*

20. *Ibid.*

21. *Territorial Papers of the U.S. Department of Interior, op. cit.*

22. *Ibid.*

23. *Ibid.*

24. Keleher, *op. cit.*

25. *Ibid.*

26. *Territorial Papers of the U.S. Department of Interior, op. cit.*

27. *Ibid.*

28. *Ibid.*

29. *Ibid.*

30. U.S. Department of Interior: *In the Matter of the Investigation, op. cit.*

31. *Territorial Papers of the U.S. Department of Interior, op. cit.*

32. Miguel A. Otero, *My Life on the Frontier, 1864-1882,* New York, Press of the Pioneers, 1935.

LEW WALLACE

TEN

Close of an Era

LEW WALLACE

1878-81

T HE PIONEERING PERIOD OF NEW MEXICO WAS COMING to a close when Lewis "Lew" Wallace accepted the governorship of New Mexico in the fall of 1878. With the Lincoln County War at its height, conditions in New Mexico that year did not foreshadow the fact that the end of outlaws and wild Indians was near.

President Rutherford B. Hayes was fortunate in obtaining Lew Wallace, a proven leader in civil and military positions, to undertake the position of chief executive of New Mexico upon the suspension of S. B. Axtell. Certainly, Lew Wallace accepted the position as a challenge, for the small salary was not sufficient for his needs. He was at work upon his new novel, *Ben-Hur,* but he must have known that most of his time would be occupied in dealing with banditry and Indian depredations.

Before coming to New Mexico, Lew Wallace—soldier, statesman, novelist—had served in the Mexican War, held the rank of major general during the Civil War, practiced law, served on a court martial concerned with the assassination of Abraham Lincoln, been chairman of the Andersonville prison inquiry, and aided the forces of Benito Juarez in Mexico.

As a youth in Indiana, Wallace's ambition was to be a painter. As governor of New Mexico, handsome Lew Wallace could be seen sketching sleeping plazas, village citizens, and grotesque characters.[1]

Even with his varied background, Lew Wallace found that being governor of New Mexico was trying. Later, he wrote, "Every calculation based on experience elsewhere fails in New Mexico."[2]

He arrived in Santa Fe on September 29, 1878, after a six-day journey from Indianapolis. The last two days he traveled by bone-breaking buckboard, covering 130 miles from Trinidad, Colorado. He was sworn in as governor by Samuel G. Parks, associate justice of the territorial supreme court, and soon dispatched a note to Axtell, enclosing the President's order of suspension. The following morning, he called upon Axtell.

Axtell did not conceal his resentment at being summarily removed; he requested two weeks before yielding up the Palace. Wallace agreed to the delay, but he made sure that Axtell understood who was now governor.[3]

Wallace spent his first three days in office poring over piles of papers and conferring with the leaders of the warring factions. He sent for them separately, questioned them, and obtained from each his account of the feud that had almost depopulated Lincoln County.[4]

Governor Wallace then forwarded to Secretary of Interior Carl Schurz in Washington reports from the Lincoln County judge, the U.S. marshal and the commandant at Fort Stanton, telling of the lawlessness in Lincoln County. In his report, Judge Warren Bristol listed his reasons against holding court in Lincoln County:

. . . first, the sheriff has either abandoned or been driven from his office or duty and taken refuge at Fort Stanton . . . a large part of the better class of the population from which jurors should be drawn have fled from the country . . . witnesses are intimidated, killed, or driven from the country. . . . There seems to be lacking that degree of force which is necessary to render the execution of the mandates of the court at all.[5]

U.S. Marshal John Sherman, Jr., wrote:

. . . Two contending factions seems to have attracted to their respective standards a lawless body of armed men who by pursuing a merciless system of retaliation and by committing murder in its most revolting form in cold blood and with a reckless disregard of human life that would disgrace savages have either driven out of that country or frightened into abject submission the remaining inhabitants who have had neither sympathy with or interest in the courses that led to the present deplorable condition. . . . in my judgment there is now no means of enforcing the law in that country without aid from United States troops. . . .[6]

Lt. Col. Nathan A. M. Dudley, commanding officer at Fort Stanton, stated:

The party of men styling themselves the wrestlers made up of renegades . . . have renewed their raiding with almost unparalleled vigor. Yesterday they attacked a party of laborers cutting hay near the ranch of Jose Chavez . . . without the least provocation killed three of the party, two of the sons of Chavez . . . none of these men have in any possible way been partisans or given their sympathy to either of the parties. They stole what horses they could find on the ranch and proceeded to another ranch south some 15 miles where they attacked another party of citizens putting three bolts into one man mortally wounding him and wounding another. . . . I respectfully and earnestly ask in the name of God and humanity that I may be allowed to use the force at my command to drive these murderers, horse thieves and escaped convicts out of the country. . . .[7]

Lew Wallace asked Secretary Schurz to speak to the President about the situation:

In my judgment nothing remains for me to do except call upon the President to exercise his Constitutional authority and declare the existence of insurrection in the County of Lincoln, place the County without loss of time under martial law, suspend the writ of habeas corpus therein, and appoint a military commission to come and hold session there for the trial and punishment of offenders. . . .[8]

The President responded on October 7, 1878, by issuing a proclamation:

I, Rutherford B. Hayes, President of the United States, do hereby admonish all good citizens of the United States, and especially of the Territory of New Mexico, against aiding, countenancing, abetting or taking part in such unlawful proceedings, and I do hereby warn all persons engaged in or connected with said obstruction of the laws to disperse and return peaceably to their respective abodes on or before noon of the thirteenth day of October. . . .[9]

Although the proclamation fell short of Wallace's recommendation, the President directed the military to be ready to use such force as might be necessary to maintain peace in New Mexico, under the direction of the governor.

Lew Wallace, acting upon authority from cabinet members in Washington, granted in an amnesty proclamation dated November 13, 1878, a general pardon for crimes committed:

> For the information of the people of the United States,
> and of the citizens of the Territory of New Mexico in espec-
> ial, the undersigned announces that the disorders lately pre-
> valent in Lincoln County in said Territory, have been hap-
> pily brought to an end . . . and that the people of Lincoln
> County may be helped more speedily to the management of
> their civil affairs . . . and to induce them to lay aside for-
> ever the divisions and feuds . . . the undersigned, by vir-
> tue of authority in him vested, further proclaims a general
> pardon for misdemeanors and offenses committed in the
> said County of Lincoln against the laws of the said Terri-
> tory in connection with the aforesaid disorders, between
> the first day of February, 1878, and the date of this pro-
> clamation. . . .[10]

The proclamation extended to officers of the United States
Army stationed in Lincoln County.

The proclamations from the President and Governor
Wallace brought peace to Lincoln County for three months.
The Santa Fe *Sentinel* of November 14, 1878, gave credit
to Lew Wallace: "The thanks of the people of New Mexico
are due Governor Wallace for the firm stand and the effective measures taken by him in this matter. . . .Peace is ours
once again and Governor Wallace has cause to congratulate
himself. . . ."[11] There was still some fighting in Lincoln
County, but Governor Wallace was taking effective measures
to bring it under control.

In mid-October, Mrs. Alexander A. McSween, widow
of the murdered Lincoln County merchant, employed Hus-
ton J. Chapman, a Las Vegas attorney, to bring to justice
the men who murdered her husband. Mrs. McSween's action
brought new trouble and death in Lincoln County.

Chapman wrote to Governor Wallace on November 27,
1878, presenting charges against Lt. Col. Nathan A. M.

Dudley, commanding officer at Fort Stanton: "I am in possession of facts which makes [sic] Col. Dudley criminally
responsible for the killing of McSween. . . ."[12]

Colonel Dudley had earlier criticized Governor Wallace's amnesty proclamation. He wrote in the Santa Fe *New
Mexican*:

> . . . I am aware that it is not within the province of
> an officer of the Army, to make suggestions to a civil func-
> tionary, occupying the high position held by yourself, much
> less criticize his official course; but when false and unjust
> accusations are made, whether against myself, or the gal-
> lant officers of my command, it becomes my duty to demand
> for them and myself a hearing, and not allow a general par-
> don to be promulgated for them or myself, for offenses that
> we know not of, and of which we feel ourselves guiltless.[13]

Governor Wallace asked Gen. Edward Hatch to remove Colonel Dudley from command at Fort Stanton. The
request was sent to Washington, where Gen. W. T. Sherman
refused it: "There is no military reason why he should be
displaced of his command at Fort Stanton. . . . If Gov.
Wallace will prefer charges against Lt. Col. Dudley, they
can be thoroughly examined and tried by the law of the
land. . . ."[14]

Then, on the night of February 18, 1879—exactly one
year from the date of the murder of Tunstall which had
begun the Lincoln County War—H. J. Chapman was murdered.

Years later, Mrs. Alexander A. McSween told Miguel
A. Otero of the shooting:

> I had a great deal of responsibility on my shoulders
> in settling my husband's and Mr. Tunstall's estates. To aid
> me, I secured a Las Vegas attorney named Chapman. He

was a one-armed man but a fearless fellow. One night he arrived in Lincoln from Las Vegas . . . to bring me the good news that Gov. Lew Wallace was strongly on our side of the conflict; he left to go over to his room, saying that he would return later. He happened to meet Jimmie Dolan, Billy Mathews, and Billy Campbell. Catching sight of Mr. Chapman, Dolan cried out: 'Here is the scrub who is trying to stir up things again over the McSween business. Let's show him a trick or two.' Then he deliberately insulted Mr. Chapman, and the next instant the three bullies discharged their pistols against an unarmed man who had only one arm. Chapman dropped dead.[15]

William H. Bonney witnessed the killing.

Upon hearing of the assassination of Chapman, Lew Wallace took immediate action. Accompanied by Gen. Edward Hatch, he left Santa Fe, March 2, 1879, for Lincoln County. There Wallace preferred charges against Colonel Dudley, arrested J. J. Dolan and some of his men, and interviewed William H. Bonney.

Wallace was able to persuade General Hatch to relieve Colonel Dudley by stating:

> I will state in general terms that it is charged here that Lt. Col. Dudley is responsible for the killing of several people in Lincoln County. I have information also connecting him with the recent murder of H. J. Chapman to the effect that he knew the man would be killed . . . and that one of the murder[er]s stated publicly that he had promised Col. Dudley to do the deed.[16]

Dudley was relieved from duty, by order of Hatch, to await a court of inquiry.

Wallace had three outlaws arrested for the murder of Chapman, and then Dolan was arrested. Four detachments of troops hunted down outlaws. By April 4, the guardhouse at Fort Stanton contained fifteen prisoners.

Wallace had an evening meeting with "Billy the Kid" while he was in Lincoln County. The governor, knowing that William Bonney had witnessed the murder of Chapman, wanted him to testify before the grand jury convening April 14. The governor then discussed Bonney with Judge John B. Wilson. Soon, Wallace received, through Judge Wilson, a letter from Bonney, dated March 13, 1879:

> . . . I was present When Mr. Chapman was Murdered and know who did it and . . . if it is in your power to Anully [sic] those indictments I hope you will do so so as to give me a chance to explain. please send me an answer telling me what you can do. . . . I have no Wish to fight any more indeed I have not raised an arm since Your proclamation. . . .[17]

Two days later, Governor Wallace wrote to Bonney.

> Come to the house of old Squire Wilson (not the lawyer) at nine (9) o'clock next Monday night alone. . . . I have authority to exempt you from prosecution if you will testify to what you say you know.
>
> The object of the meeting at Squire Wilson's is to arrange the matter in a way to make your life safe. To do that the utmost secrecy is to be used. *So come alone.* Don't tell anybody—not a living soul—where you are coming or the object. If you could trust Jesse Evans, you can trust me.[18]

The meeting between the young outlaw and the distinguished governor took place in Squire Wilson's home on the night of March 17, 1879, at nine o'clock. After some preliminaries, the governor and the young outlaw got down to business. It was arranged that Bonney was to be arrested, supposedly against his will. He would be held under guard, for his protection, so he could testify before the grand jury. Wallace added the solemn assurance that, in return for his testimony, Bonney would be given a pardon for his misdeeds.[19] The principal charge at that time against Bonney was the murder of Sheriff Brady.

William Bonney submitted to the arranged arrest on March 23, although those whom he was to testify against in the Chapman murder had escaped jail. Bonney knew they would seize any opportunity to kill him to prevent his testimony.

The Lincoln County grand jury convened April 14, 1879. Bonney faithfully kept the promise he made to Governor Wallace to appear and testify to law violations in Lincoln County. He testified that Dudley's troops and the sheriff's men had killed McSween's men on July 19, 1878. Colonel Dudley was indicted for arson in the burning of the McSween home, but a jury later found him not guilty.

Indictments were returned against Marion Turner and John Jones for killing McSween: " . . . with certain guns then and there loaded and charged with gunpowder shot and sent forth against the said Alexander A. McSween, in and upon the breasts and belly of him, inflicting mortal wounds from which he instantly died."[20]

Many of those indicted appeared before Judge Bristol, pleading immunity from prosecution under Governor Wallace's November 13, 1878, proclamation of amnesty. Wallace wrote to the Secretary of Interior: "They found nearly 200 indictments in the county of a voting population 150 total."[21]

Wallace returned to Santa Fe April 18, 1879, but he soon returned to Lincoln to testify in the Dudley court of inquiry. The governor was on the witness stand for five days, but only his testimony of his personal knowledge was ad-

missible. Wallace was compelled to admit that many of his
charges were based upon hearsay, that none of the witnesses
he had examined would sign affidavits. Wallace denounced
the proceedings of the court of inquiry to Secretary Schurz.

When Wallace returned to Lincoln County for the
court of inquiry, he brought his wife. They stayed at the
post trader's house at Fort Stanton. To her son Henry, Susan
E. Wallace wrote, on May 11, 1879:

> MY DEAR—General Sherman was right. We should have
> another war with Old Mexico to make her take back New
> Mexico. I did not think anything could make me think well
> of Santa Fe, but this hideous spot does. . . .
>
> The Lincoln County reign of terror is not over, and we
> hold our lives at the mercy of desperadoes and outlaws,
> chief among them "Billy the Kid" whose boast is that he
> has killed a man for every year of his life. Once he was cap-
> tured, and escaped after overpowering his guard, and now
> he swears when he has killed the sheriff and the judge who
> passed sentence upon him, and Governor Wallace, he will
> surrender and be hanged. "I mean to ride into the plaza at
> Santa Fe, hitch my horse in front of the palace, and put a
> bullet through Lew Wallace."
>
> These are his words.
>
> One of my friends warned me to close the shutters at
> evening, so the bright light of the student's-lamp might not
> make such a shining mark of the governor writing till late
> on Ben Hur. . . .[22]

After testifying before the court of inquiry, William
Bonney failed to stand trial for his old charges as he had
agreed to do on promise of the governor's pardon. He
seemed to have lost faith in Governor Wallace's assurances
to him.

Even though there was some unfinished business in

Lincoln County, Lew Wallace reported in his message to the legislature, in January 1880:

> Upon my coming into the Territory somewhat more than a year ago there were disturbances in Lincoln county occasioned by bands of lawless men who went about committing atrocities so great that the President was impelled to formally proclaim a condition of insurrection in that region. It gives me satisfaction to inform you . . . that peace is restored there.

Wallace asked for legislative apportionment, funds to pay the small public debt ($15,181.02), revision of the laws, redrafting of the criminal code, provisions for better public schools, and the enforced teaching of English. Wallace spoke of the Indian problem:

> It is my duty to speak of the recent Indian outbreaks with a view to a recommendation which is common with all thoughtful persons in the Territory. . . . The President in his recent message is happy in the belief that a better day is about to dawn upon the relations between the government and the Indians. . . . As his recommendations were general and without exception, they came upon the people of New Mexico in a most unfortunate time; the blood of the freighters—the genuine freighters—was not yet washed from the stones upon the hill between Mason's ranche [sic] and Fort Cummings; the people of Doña Ana and Grant counties, summing up their dead at the hands of Victorio, had reached 100 men, women, and children, and the count was still going on. So it is not strange if, in great bitterness of spirit, New Mexicans, without regard to class or nativity, are disposed to believe that the President reflects the sentimentalism of which gentle folks on the banks of the Hudson and in hearing of the bells of Cambridge are the supposed best representatives. The latter are situated happily for the

indulgence of rose-colored theories about the Indians. . . .

It is the common opinion in our Territory that there is but one course for us to pursue, and that is to get ready to defend ourselves. . . .[23]

The outbreak of the Indian war occurred in the spring of 1877 when federal troops drove 450 Apaches from their reservation at Ojo Caliente, New Mexico, to a desolate wasteland 200 miles west in southeastern Arizona. Susan Wallace wrote:

The reason assigned by our Government for the removal from this spot to the arid volcanic mesa of Arizona was that . . . two agencies might be consolidated, and the expense of maintaining them lessened. . . . Their war chief was Victorio, successor to the renowned Magnus Colorado. . . .[24]

The legislature gave the governor authority to call out and organize a force of volunteers, not to exceed 1000 in number, for the protection of the lives and property of the citizens. The sum of $100,000 was appropriated for the militia.

Secretary of War Alexander Ramsey advised Wallace:

If the Territory of New Mexico calls a thousand men for defense of her scattered settlements, the Governor should be notified that the territory must pay and provide for them. . . . The Comanches are in the custody of an authorized agent in the Indian Territory, more than a thousand miles from the Guadalupe Mountains of south New Mexico. . . .[25]

Wallace replied:

I will hasten preparations to execute the law just passed giving me men and money for defense against the Indians. As to the Comanches being more than a thousand miles from the Guadalupe Mountains of south New Mexico, people in Alabama will be astonished to hear that they have such an addition to their population.[26]

In March 1880, Lew Wallace spoke of the strategy of the Indian leader:

> Last year an Apache chief, Victorio, a man seventy-five years old, became hostile and took to the war-path. In some respects he is a wonderful man, and, commencing with a band of seventy-five warriors, he succeeded in uniting tribes always hostile to one another before, and in a few weeks he had three hundred well-armed followers. He has held his own against us from that day to this, in open conflict, and he has murdered about one hundred men, women, and children in the most horrible manner. He is an enemy not to be despised.[27]

Susan Wallace wrote:

> [Before the war ended] more than 400 white persons were scalped and tortured to death with devilish ingenuity. . . .
>
> The Apache love of meat is not fastidious, and they are fond of mule and horse flesh. Deer, antelope—whatever the game may be—every portion except the bones, is consumed, the entrails being an especial delicacy. They partially cook it, generally eating it extremely rare. . . .[28]

Near the end of October, Governor Wallace hurried to Ojo Caliente, which had suffered several Apache raids. It was a dangerous trip and the people were very appreciative of the governor's concern for them. They showed him the latest toll. Before the altar of the church were "sixteen corpses, men, women, and children, some of them shockingly mutilated."[29]

Victorio was killed in Mexico in October 1880, ending

the worst of the Apache wars, although new leaders arose—
Nana and, later, Geronimo—who continued raiding until
1886, when the Apaches were finally subdued.

In October 1880, for the first time in New Mexico history, a President of the United States visited the territory.

Rutherford B. Hayes, his wife and a small party, returning from a visit to California, rode to the terminus of the
Southern Pacific railroad in Grant County. Accompanied by
a small military escort, the party boarded ambulances for
the trip to Santa Fe. After a journey of several days, during
which they camped out, the party arrived in Santa Fe on
Thursday, October 28, 1880.[30]

As reported in the Santa Fe *Weekly Democrat,* the
President addressed the crowd which gathered in Santa Fe:

> Naturally enough everyone is interested to see an an-
> cient capital like this. I believe it is claimed by intelligent
> people here that Santa Fe is the oldest town in the United
> States; that it was settled before St. Augustine; before our
> forefathers founded Plymouth rock or the cavaliers settled
> in Virginia. . . .

Throughout Lew Wallace's stay in New Mexico, he was
interested in acquiring good mining property. He prepared
a "Report of the Governor of New Mexico" in 1879 on the
possible development of New Mexico. In it, he said:

> There are three interests in New Mexico worth con-
> sideration: the mineral, the grazing or pastoral, and the
> agricultural. . . .
> Putting the soil, river, and climate together, the Rio
> Grande Valley is more nearly a duplication of the region
> of the Nile than any other of which I have knowledge. . . .
> I am of the opinion that New Mexico will come quite up
> with her neighbors in the yield of precious metals. A variety

of causes have heretofore contributed to prevent her thorough exploration for such wealth. . . . A Pueblo [Indian] might be induced to part with his eye-teeth; no inducement could prevail upon him to take a white man to a mine. . . .[31]

Immediately after arriving in New Mexico in the fall of 1878, Governor Wallace explored the Spanish silver mines east of Bernalillo. The following year he acquired claims in the Los Cerrillos area, twenty miles from Santa Fe. He and his son Henry acquired claims in Socorro, Grant, and San Miguel counties. At one time, Governor Wallace offered his holdings for several hundred thousand dollars, but eventually dropped the price. In later life, he returned to New Mexico, hoping for a profit from his holdings—a profit which never came. In 1882, through his attorney in Santa Fe, Wallace sold a mining claim to L. Bradford Prince.[32]

In the winter of 1880, after a year of peace and calm, Wallace's attention again was called to Lincoln County and William Bonney. The paths of Governor Wallace and Bonney crossed again in December 1880. Bonney, with other outlaws, stole some horses and was charged with murdering a deputy sheriff. Bonney wrote to the governor on December 12, 1880, pleading innocent of killing the deputy, and asserting that the deputy had been killed by his own men when they mistook him for Bonney.

Governor Wallace did not answer Bonney's letter. Instead, in December 1880, he offered a $500 reward for the "delivery of Bonney, alias 'The Kid' to the Sheriff of Lincoln County." Bonney was captured December 23 with two others. He was taken to Las Vegas, and later transferred to Santa Fe.

From the Santa Fe jail, Bonney wrote the governor four times, early in 1881:

[January 1] I would like to see you for a few moments if you can spare time.

[March 2] I wish you would come down to the jail to see me. It will be to your interest to come and see me.

[March 4] . . . I expect you have forgotten what you promised me this month two years ago, but I have not. . . . I have done everything that I promised you I would and you have done nothing that you promised me. . . .

[March 27] . . . for the *last* time I ask. Will you keep your promise. I start below tomorrow. . . .[33]

Bonney received no reply to his notes. Apparently the governor, who earlier had promised him a pardon for the killing of Sheriff Brady, felt that Bonney's later crimes cancelled his agreement.

In April 1881, at Mesilla, Bonney was convicted of the murder of Sheriff William Brady in Lincoln on April 1, 1878, and was sentenced to death.

The Mesilla *News*, April 15, quoted an interview with Bonney:

> Considering the active part Governor Wallace took on our side and the friendly relations that existed between him and me, and the promise he made me, I think he ought to pardon me. Don't know that he will do it. When I was arrested for that murder he let me out and gave me the freedom of the town. . . .

On April 30, 1881, Governor Wallace signed the death warrant for William Bonney, setting the execution date for Friday, May 13; the execution was to be by hanging.

But the death warrant was to prove useless, for two days earlier, April 28, Bonney had snatched a pistol from his guard in the Lincoln County jail. He shot and killed both his guards and rode away. The governor again offered a $500 reward for the capture of Bonney.

After April 28, Bonney lived the life of a hunted man. For twelve weeks he roamed the area until, finally, at Fort Sumner late in the evening, July 14, 1881, at Peter Maxwell's home, Bonney was shot by Sheriff Pat Garrett.

Lew Wallace, gifted writer, managed to find time for the work he loved while serving as governor of troubled New Mexico. He wrote to his wife, Susan:

> Just returned from the ride. How delicious it was— What perfection of air and sunlight! And what a landscape discovered to show you when you come—a picture to make the fame of an artist, could he only put on canvas as it is! Soft blue sky, vast distance, bounded by purple walls as transparent and summery, it is hard to believe it. . . . The sun goes down gradually in tinted clouds, which hover over the long purple mountain ranges, for as there are mountains in the east so there are mountains in the west—mountains, understand, not hills, royal mountains, in view of which one knows the delight Ruskin writes about. Upon the going out of the day, the wind dies, leaving the night still and cool, and gradually growing cooler until at midnight if you are out of doors, you want a heavy shawl, while if you are indoors, a fire is cheery and enjoyable.[34]

During his stay in New Mexico, Wallace worked at every opportunity to finish his novel, *Ben-Hur*. He wrote to his wife:

> I am busy putting in every spare minute copying my book for publication. It is curious this jumping from the serious things of life to the purely romantic. It is like nothing so much as living two lives in one. To pass from a meeting of the Wise Men in the Desert to effecting a recon-

ciliation in the legislature and breaking a deadlock, are
certainly wide enough apart.[35]

On another occasion, he wrote to Susan:

> I note your criticisms of the march to Golgotha, and
> am of the opinion that they are all just. Some of them I had
> in mind with intentions to correct them. . . . One day I
> wrote from ten a.m. to ten p.m. I have so many and all sorts
> of interruptions in this land of ample leisure. I am trying
> to do four things: first, manage a legislature of most jealous
> elements; second, take care of an Indian war; third, finish
> a book; fourth, sell some mines. Can you fancy a greater
> diversity of occupations?[36]

Wallace described the Palace of the Governors and his
work on *Ben-Hur*:

> Everybody has heard of the Old Palace in Santa Fe,
> New Mexico. A rambling, one-story adobe structure, with
> walls in places six feet thick. . . . The walls were grimy,
> the undressed boards of the floor rested flat upon the
> ground; the cedar rafters, rainstained . . . and over-
> weighted by tons and tons of mud composing the roof. . . .
> Nevertheless, in that cavernous chamber I wrote the eighth
> and last book of Ben-Hur.
>
> My custom when night came was to lock the doors and
> bolt the windows of the office proper, and with a student's-
> lamp, bury myself in the four soundless walls of the forbid-
> ding annex . . . there, at my rough pine table, the Count
> of Monte Cristo in his dungeon of stone was not more lost
> to the world.
>
> The ghosts, if they were ever about, did not disturb
> me; yet in the hush of that gloomy harborage I beheld the
> Crucifixion, and strove to write what I beheld. . . . Long
> before I was through with my book, I became a believer in
> God and Christ.[37]

As Lew Wallace labored to complete *Ben-Hur,* the major event of the century was taking place in New Mexico —the completion of two great transcontinental railroads, the Southern Pacific and the Atchison, Topeka and Santa Fe, that would bridge the territory.

The New Mexico legislature, in February 1880, passed a resolution:

> The Legislature of New Mexico observes with pleasure and satisfaction the completion of a line of railroad to the city of Santa Fe. . . . This event may well be regarded as the most important in the history of the Territory, and as the beginning of a new era. . . .[38]

The last spikes completing the Southern Pacific Branch to Santa Fe were driven by Gen. Edward Hatch, Chief Justice L. Bradford Prince and Lew Wallace.

The sub-head of a Santa Fe *New Mexican* story February 14, 1880, read: "And the Old Santa Fe Trail Passes into Oblivion."

The Atchison, Topeka and Santa Fe reached Albuquerque April 22, 1880. The Atchison, Topeka and Santa Fe and the Southern Pacific joined at Deming on March 10, 1881, forming the first all-rail route across New Mexico.[39]

March 9, 1881, Lew Wallace wrote to the Secretary of Interior:

> You will do me the favor to take notice of the accompanying paper and submit it to the President:
> "It gives me pleasure to report New Mexico in a state of quiet. A large immigration is pouring into it under inducement of rich mineral discoveries and increased railroad facilities . . . it will be in condition to become a state before the expiration of the administration just inaugurated. . . ."[40]

On the same date, Wallace wrote President James A. Garfield, for whom he had campaigned in the fall of 1880, offering his resignation: "I respectfully offer you my resignation, remarking that if it should be your pleasure to continue me in the office, I will do my best, as heretofore, to discharge its duties satisfactorily. . . ."[41]

Lew Wallace appeared, soon thereafter, to lose interest in New Mexico. He wrote to his wife: "I confess I am getting very tired of this office. There is nobody here who cares for me, and nobody I care for."[42] And again to Susan: "I wish my successor, whoever he be, was come. Of course he will do just as I did, have the same ideas, make the same attempts, and with the same heartiness of effort, soon cool in zeal, then finally say, 'All right, let her drift.' "[43]

Lew Wallace left Santa Fe, May 30, 1881, for Crawfordsville, Indiana. He departed Santa Fe in a Pullman car and his departure marked the beginning of a new era, for he had arrived three years earlier in a horse-drawn stagecoach.

The new territorial governor, Lionel A. Sheldon, arrived June 4, 1881.

In summing up, the newspapers of New Mexico praised Lew Wallace's administration—an administration that saw the elimination of outlaws and wild Indians. Said the Las Vegas *Optic,* on March 23, 1881: " . . . We believe Gov. Wallace to be almost the only respectable and worthy gentleman who was ever appointed to a Federal Office in New Mexico." The Las Cruces *Semi-Weekly,* March 30, 1881, stated: "Gov. Wallace . . . has made the best executive New Mexico has had for many years. . . . He has been the governor during his entire term, and we honor him for it."

Lew Wallace, although scaling the heights of fame with his novel, *Ben-Hur,* and serving as minister to Turkey under Garfield, never completely forgot New Mexico. He came back to the territory from time to time in connection with mining business.

In 1889, Lew Wallace wrote L. Bradford Prince, denying that he had offered $500 for an interview with William Bonney: "Only Squire Wilson helped, and he rendered the help without reward or the promise thereof."[44]

In 1902, Wallace wrote the regents of the Smithsonian Institute in Washington, D.C., recommending that the agency take over the Palace of the Governors in Santa Fe because of its historical interest.

On February 15, 1905, Lew Wallace "bade this world good-night—his dreaming ended. He had found the New World, the universal religion, the One God."[45]

NOTES

1. Wallace's pencil sketch of the Palace of Governors, Santa Fe, was used in a book, *Land of the Pueblos*, by his wife, Susan E. Wallace. It is reproduced on the endsheets of the present volume.

2. Irving McKee, *'Ben Hur' Wallace, the Life of General Lew Wallace*, Berkeley, Univ. of California Press, 1947.

3. *Ibid.*

4. Lew Wallace, *An Autobiography*, v. II, New York, Harper, 1906.

5. Museum of New Mexico Library, *Items Dealing with General Lew Wallace's Years as Governor of New Mexico Territory, 1878-1881*, with a few earlier New Mexico Items, from the Wallace Collection, William Henry Smith Memorial Library, Indiana Historical Society.

6. *Territorial Papers of the U.S. Department of Interior*, New Mexico, 1851-1914, Executive Proceedings, Oct. 8, 1874—Dec. 21, 1888.

7. Museum of New Mexico Library, *op. cit.*

8. *Territorial Papers of the U.S. Department of Interior, op. cit.*

9. Phillip Rasch, "Exit Axtell—Enter Wallace," *New Mexico Historical Review*, v. XXXII, July 1957.

10. *Territorial Papers of the U.S. Department of Interior, op. cit.*

11. Historian Ralph E. Twitchell gave Wallace no credit, saying that the so-called war had practically ceased three months before Wallace's arrival. *Old Santa Fe, The Story of New Mexico's Ancient Capital*, Santa Fe, New Mexico Publishing Corp., 1925.

12. Museum of New Mexico Library, *op. cit.*

13. William A. Keleher, *Violence in Lincoln County, 1869-1881, A New Mexico Item*, Albuquerque, Univ. of New Mexico Press, 1957.

14. *Ibid.*

15. Miguel A. Otero, *The Real Billy the Kid, with New Light on the Lincoln County War*, New York, R. R. Wilson, 1936.

16. Keleher, *op. cit.*

17. *Ibid.*

18. William Lee Hamlin, *The True Story of Billy the Kid*, Caldwell, Caxton, 1959 (item from Indiana Historical Society, reproduced).

19. McKee, *op. cit.*

20. Keleher, *op. cit.*

21. *Territorial Papers of the U.S. Department of Interior, op. cit.*

22. Susan E. Wallace, *The Land of the Pueblos,* Troy, Nims & Knight, 1889.

23. *Territorial Papers of the U.S. Department of Interior, op. cit.*

24. Susan E. Wallace, *op. cit.*

25. Lew Wallace, *op. cit.*

26. *Ibid.*

27. *Ibid.*

28. Susan E. Wallace, *op. cit.*

29. Lew Wallace, *op. cit.*

30. *Territorial Papers of the U.S. Department of Interior, op. cit.*

31. *Reports of the Governors of Arizona, Dakota, Idaho, Montana, New Mexico, Utah and Washington Territories, Made to the Secretary of the Interior, 1879,* Washington, Government Printing Office, 1879.

32. *Lew Wallace Papers,* State Records Center, Archives Division, Santa Fe.

33. Hamlin, *op. cit.*

34. Keleher, *op. cit.*

35. Lew Wallace, *op. cit.*

36. *Ibid.*

37. *Ibid.*

38. William A. Keleher, *The Fabulous Frontier, Twelve New Mexico Items* (rev. ed.), Albuquerque, Univ. of New Mexico Press, 1962.

39. Ralph E. Twitchell, *The Leading Facts of New Mexican History,* v. II, Cedar Rapids, Torch, 1912.

40. *Territorial Papers of the U.S. Department of Interior, op. cit.*

41. Keleher, *Violence in Lincoln County, op. cit.*

42. McKee, *op. cit.*

43. *Ibid.*

44. *Lew Wallace Papers,* State Records Center, *op. cit.*

45. Lew Wallace, *op. cit.*

Bibliography

Abel, Annie Heloise. "Indian Affairs in New Mexico Under the Administration of William Carr Lane." *New Mexico Historical Review,* Vol. 16, July 1941.

Abel, Annie Heloise, ed. *The Official Correspondence of James S. Calhoun while Indian Agent at Santa Fe and Superintendent of Indian Affairs in New Mexico 1849-52.* Washington: 1915.

Abert, James W. *Abert's New Mexico Report 1846-47.* Albuquerque: Horn & Wallace, 1962.

Abraham Rencher Papers. Chapel Hill: University of North Carolina Library.

Anderson, Arthur J. O. "Santa Fe on Bandelier's First Visit." *El Palacio,* Vol. 54, May 1947.

Anderson, George B. *History of New Mexico.* Los Angeles: Pacific States Publishing Co., 1907.

Appleton's Cyclopedia of American Biography, James Grant Wilson and John Fiske, eds. New York: D. Appleton and Co., 1888.

Arnold, Elliot. *The Time of the Gringo.* New York: Alfred A. Knopf, 1953.

Bancroft, Hubert Howe. *History of Arizona and New Mexico, 1530-1888.* San Francisco: History Co., 1889. Facsimile edition, Albuquerque: Horn & Wallace, 1962.

Beck, Warren A. *New Mexico, A History of Four Centuries.* Norman: University of Oklahoma Press, 1962.

Bender, A. B. "Frontier Defense in the Territory of New Mexico, 1846-1853, 1853-1861." *New Mexico Historical Review,* Vol. 9, July, Oct. 1934.

Bender, A. B. *The March of Empire: Frontier Defense in the Southwest, 1848-1860.* Lawrence: University of Kansas, 1952.

Bennett, James A. *Forts and Forays—James A. Bennett: A dragoon in New Mexico, 1850-1856.* Clinton E. Brooks and Frank D. Reeve, eds. Albuquerque: University of New Mexico Press, 1948.

Bieber, R. P. "Letters of William Carr Lane, 1852-1854." *New Mexico Historical Review,* Vol. 3, April 1928.

Biographical Directory of the American Congress, 1774-1949, The Continental Congress and the Congress of the United States. Washington: Government Printing Office, 1950.

Bloom, Lansing B., ed. "Historical Society Minutes, 1859-1863." *New Mexico Historical Review,* Vol. 18, July 1943.

Bloom, Lansing B., ed. "Bourke on the Southwest." *New Mexico Historical Review,* Vol. 10, Oct. 1935.

Bloom, Lansing B., and Donnelly, Thomas C. *New Mexico History and Civics.* Albuquerque: The University Press, 1933.

Book of Clear Record of the Legislative Council of the Territory of New Mexico, Dec. 1, 1851, to Jan. 30, 1856. Bound ms. Santa Fe: State Records Center.

Bratton, Sam Gilbert. *New Mexico: Mythology, Tradition, History.* 71st Congress, 2nd session, Senate Document 147. Rev. by Dorothy Woodward. Washington: Government Printing Office, 1930.

Carson, Christopher. *Kit Carson's Own Story of His Life as Dictated to Col. and Mrs. D. C. Peters about 1856-57 and never before Published.* Blanche C. Grant, ed. Taos: 1926.

Clarke, Dwight L. *Stephen Watts Kearny, Soldier of the West.* Norman: University of Oklahoma Press, 1961.

Coan, Charles F. *A History of New Mexico,* Chicago: The American Historical Society, 1925.

Cooke, P. St. George. *The Conquest of New Mexico and California: an Historical and Personal Narrative.* New York: G. P. Putnam's Sons, 1878.

Coulter, Ellis Merton. *The Confederate States of America, 1861-1865.* Baton Rouge: Louisiana State University Press, 1950.

Curry, George. *George Curry 1861-1947: An Autobiography.* H. B. Hening, ed. Albuquerque: University of New Mexico Press, 1958.

Cutts, James Madison. *The Conquest of California and New Mexico by the Forces of the United States in the Years 1846-1847.* Philadelphia: Carey & Hart, 1847.

Dargan, Lena. *James S. Calhoun in New Mexico.* Unpublished Master's thesis. Albuquerque: University of New Mexico, 1932.

Davis, William Watts Hart. *El Gringo: or New Mexico and Her People.* Santa Fe: Rydal Press, 1938.

Donnell, F. S. "When Las Vegas was the Capital of New Mexico." *New Mexico Historical Review,* Vol. 8, Oct. 1933.

Drumm, Stella M. *Letters of William Carr Lane 1819-1831—Glimpses of the Past.* Missouri Historical Society, ed. St. Louis: Jefferson Memorial, 1940.

Espinosa, J. Manuel, ed. "Memoir of a Kentuckian in New Mexico, 1848-84." *New Mexico Historical Review,* Vol. 13, Jan. 1938.

Executive Documents Printed by Order of the House of Representatives. 38th Congress, 1st session, 1863-64, Vol. 3, Nos. 41-42.

Fergusson, Erna. *New Mexico: A Pageant of Three Peoples.* New York: Alfred A. Knopf, 1951.

Fergusson, Erna. *Our Southwest.* New York: Alfred A. Knopf, 1940.

Fergusson, Harvey. *Rio Grande.* New York: Alfred A. Knopf, 1936.

Fitzpatrick, George, ed. *This is New Mexico.* Albuquerque: Horn & Wallace, 1962.

Fulton, Maurice Garland, and Horgan, Paul. *New Mexico's Own Chronicle; Three Races in the Writings of Four Hundred Years.* Dallas: Banks, Upshaw, 1937.

Ganaway, Loomis Morton. *New Mexico and the Sectional Controversy, 1846-1861.* Albuquerque: University of New Mexico Press, 1944.

Garber, Paul Neff. *The Gadsden Treaty.* Philadelphia: University of Pennsylvania Press, 1923.

Green, Fletcher M. "James S. Calhoun: Pioneer Georgia Leader and First Governor of New Mexico." *Georgia Historical Quarterly,* Dec. 1955.

Gregg, Josiah. *Commerce of the Prairies.* Max Moorhead, ed. Norman: University of Oklahoma Press, 1954.

Gregg, Josiah. *Diary and Letters.* Norman: University of Oklahoma Press, 1941-44.

Griggs, George. *History of Mesilla Valley or The Gadsden Purchase Known in Mexico as the Treaty of Mesilla.* Mesilla: The Author, 1930.

Haines, Helen. *History of New Mexico from the Spanish Conquest to the Present Time, 1530-1890.* New York: New Mexico Historical Publishing Co., 1891.

Hall, Martin Hardwick. *Sibley's New Mexico Campaign.* Austin: University of Texas Press, 1960.

Hamlin, William Lee. *The True Story of Billy the Kid.* Caldwell: Caxton, 1959.

Hammond, George P., and Donnelly, Thomas C. *The Story of New Mexico, Its History and Government.* Albuquerque: University of New Mexico Press, 1936.

Hepler, Robert Daniel. *William Watts Davis in New Mexico.* Unpublished Master's thesis. Albuquerque: University of New Mexico, 1941.

The Historical Encyclopedia of New Mexico. Ellis Arthur Davis, ed. Albuquerque: New Mexico Historical Association, 1945.

Horgan, Paul. *Great River: The Rio Grande in North American History.* New York: Rinehart, 1954.

Horn, Calvin, and Wallace, William S., eds. *Confederate Victories in the Southwest, Prelude to Defeat.* Albuquerque: Horn & Wallace, 1961.

Horn, Calvin, and Wallace, William S., eds. *Union Army Operations in the Southwest, Final Victory.* Albuquerque: Horn & Wallace, 1961.

Hughes, John T. *Doniphan's Expedition, Containing an Account of the Conquest of New Mexico.* Cincinnati: J. A. & V. P. James, 1850.

Hunt, Aurora. *Major General James Henry Carleton 1814-1873, Western Frontier Dragoon.* Glendale: Arthur H. Clark Co., 1958.

Inman, Henry. *The Old Santa Fe Trail; The Story of a Great Highway.* Topeka: Crane, 1916.

Items Dealing with General Lew Wallace's Years as Governor of New Mexico Territory, 1878-1881, with a few earlier New Mexico Items. From the Wallace Collection, William Henry Smith Memorial Library, Indiana Historical Society. Santa Fe: Museum of New Mexico Library.

Johnson, J. Stoddard. *Memorial History of Louisville.* Vol. I. No pub.

Keleher, William A. *The Fabulous Frontier, Twelve New Mexico Items.* Rev. ed. Albuquerque: University of New Mexico Press, 1962.

Keleher, William A. *Maxwell Land Grant, A New Mexico Item.* Santa Fe: Rydal Press, 1942.

Keleher, William A. *Turmoil in New Mexico 1846-1868.* Santa Fe: Rydal Press, 1952.

Keleher, William A. *Violence in Lincoln County, 1869-1881, A New Mexico Item.* Albuquerque: University of New Mexico Press, 1957.

Kerby, Robert Lee. *The Confederate Invasion of New Mexico and Arizona 1861-1862.* Los Angeles: Westernlore Press, 1958.

Lavender, David. *Bent's Fort.* New York, 1952.

Laws of the Territory of New Mexico, Passed by the Legislative Assembly, 1856-57. Printed at the Office of the Democrat, 1857.

Lew Wallace Papers. Santa Fe: State Records Center.

Loyola, Sister Mary. "The American Occupation of New Mexico, 1821-1852." *New Mexico Historical Review,* Vol. 14, July 1939.

McKee, Irving. *"Ben Hur" Wallace, the Life of General Lew Wallace.* Berkeley: University of California Press, 1947.

Magoffin, Susan Shelby. *Down the Santa Fe Trail and into Mexico. The Diary of Susan Shelby Magoffin, 1846-1847.* Stella M. Drumm, ed. New Haven: Yale University Press, 1926.

Meriwether Letters. Albuquerque: University of New Mexico Library.

Minor, Louisa H. A. *The Meriwethers and Their Connections.* Charlottesville: University of Virginia, 1892.

Mitchell, W. A. "Historic Linn." From *La Cyge Weekly Journal,* Collections of the Kansas State Historical Society, 1923-25, ed. by William Elsey Connelly. Topeka: Kansas State, 1925.

The National Cyclopaedia of American Biography, being the His-tory of the United States. New York: James T. White and Co., 1898.

Otero, Miguel Antonio. *My Life on the Frontier, 1864-1882.* New York: Press of the Pioneers, 1935.

Otero, Miguel Antonio. *The Real Billy the Kid, with New Light on the Lincoln County War.* New York: R. R. Wilson, 1936.

Pearce, T. M., and Hendon, Telfair, eds. *America in the Southwest; A Regional Anthology.* Albuquerque: The University Press, 1933.

Poldervaart, Arie W. *Black-Robed Justice.* Santa Fe: Historical Society of New Mexico, 1948.

Poldervaart, Arie W. "The New Mexico Law Library—A History." *New Mexico Historical Review,* Vol. 21, Jan. 1946.

Prince, L. Bradford. *A Concise History of New Mexico.* Cedar Rapids: Torch Press, 1912.

Prince, L. Bradford. *Historical Sketches of New Mexico from the Earliest Records to the American Occupation.* Kansas City: Ramsey, Millet and Hudson, 1883.

Prince, L. Bradford. *New Mexico's Struggle for Statehood, Sixty Years of Effort to Obtain Self Government.* Santa Fe: New Mex-ican Printing Co., 1910.

Putnam, George Haven. *Abraham Lincoln; the People's Leader in the Struggle for National Existence.* New York: G. P. Putnam's Sons, 1909.

Rasch, Phillip. "Exit Axtell—Enter Wallace." *New Mexico Histor-ical Review,* Vol. 32, July 1957.

Read, Benjamin Maurice. *A Treatise on the Disputed Points of the History of New Mexico.* Santa Fe: The Author, 1919.

Records of the U.S. House of Representatives, Credentials of Mem-bers, 21st Congress. Credentials of Abraham Rencher, R. G. 233. Washington: National Archives.

Reeve, Frank D. "The Federal Indian Policy of New Mexico." *New Mexico Historical Review,* Vol. 12, July 1937.

Reeve, Frank D. "The Government and the Navaho, 1846-1858." *New Mexico Historical Review,* Vol. 14, Jan. 1939.

Reeve, Frank D. *History of New Mexico.* Vol. 2. New York: Lewis Historical Publishing Co., 1961.

Rittenhouse, Jack D. *New Mexico Civil War Bibliography 1861-1865; an annotated checklist of books and pamphlets.* Houston: Stagecoach Press, 1960.

The Robert Todd Lincoln Collection of the Papers of Abraham Lincoln, 1790-1916. Washington: National Archives.

Rodriguez, Arnold L. "New Mexico in Transition." *New Mexico Historical Review,* Vol. 24, July 1949.

Sabin, Edwin Legrand. *Kit Carson Days, 1809-1868; Adventures in the Path of Empire.* Rev. ed. New York: Press of the Pioneers, 1935.

Sanchez, George I. *Forgotten People: A Study of New Mexicans.* Albuquerque: University of New Mexico Press, 1940.

"Santa Fe in Notes and Documents." *New Mexico Historical Review,* Vol. 25, Jan. 1950.

Saunders, Lyle. *A Guide to Materials Bearing on Cultural Relations in New Mexico.* Albuquerque: University of New Mexico Press, 1940.

Stephen, Leslie, and Lee, Sidney, eds. *Dictionary of National Biography.* London: Smith, Elder & Co., 1908.

Twitchell, Ralph Emerson. *Historical Sketch of Governor William Carr Lane.* Santa Fe: Historical Society of New Mexico, Publication 20, 1917.

Twitchell, Ralph Emerson. *The History of the Military Occupation of the Territory of New Mexico, from 1846 to 1851 by the Government of the United States.* Denver: Smith-Brooks Co., 1909.

Twitchell, Ralph Emerson. *The Leading Facts of New Mexican History.* Vol. 2. Cedar Rapids: Torch Press, 1912.

Twitchell, Ralph Emerson. *Old Santa Fe: The Story of New Mexico's Ancient Capital.* Santa Fe: New Mexico Publishing Co., 1925.

Twitchell, Ralph Emerson. *The Spanish Archives of New Mexico.* Cedar Rapids: Torch Press, 1914.

Twitchell, Ralph Emerson. *The Story of the Conquest of Santa Fe, New Mexico, and the Building of Old Fort Marcy, A.D. 1846.* Santa Fe: Historical Society of New Mexico, Publication 24, 1923.

U.S. Congress. *The Congressional Globe: New Series.* Debates and Proceedings of 30th Congress, by Blair and Rives. Vols. 18, 19. Washington: Blair & Rives, 1848.

U.S. Department of the Interior. *In the Matter of the Investigation of Charges against S. B. Axtell, Governor of New Mexico.* 1875-1882. Washington: National Archives.

U.S. Department of the Interior. *Reports of the Governors of Arizona, Dakota, Idaho, Montana, New Mexico, Utah and Washington Territories.* Washington: Government Printing Office, 1879.

U.S. Department of the Interior. *Territorial Papers of the U.S. Department of Interior.* New Mexico, 1851-1914. Washington: National Archives.

U.S. Department of the Interior, Appointments Division. *Selected Documents pertaining to S. B. Axtell and Lew Wallace, Governors of the Territory of New Mexico, 1875-1882.* Washington: National Archives.

U.S. Department of State. *General Records of the Department of State, Miscellaneous Letters Series.* Aug. 13, 1853—May 22, 1856, Meriwether correspondence. Washington: National Archives.

U.S. Office of Indian Affairs. *Records of the New Mexico Superintendency of Indian Affairs, 1849-80.* Washington: National Archives.

U.S. War Department, *Letters sent, Military affairs 1800-1861.* Washington: National Archives.

Vaughn, John H. *History and Government of New Mexico.* Las Cruces: New Mexico State College, 1921.

Vaughn, John H. "Preliminary Report of the Archives of New Mexico." *Annual Report,* American Historical Association, 1909.

Waldrip, William I. *New Mexico during the Civil War.* Unpublished Master's thesis. Albuquerque: University of New Mexico, 1950.

Walker, Charles S. "Causes of the Confederate Invasion of New Mexico." *New Mexico Historical Review,* Vol. 8, April, 1933.

Wallace, Isabel. *Life and Letters of General W. H. L. Wallace.* Chicago: R. R. Donnelley & Sons, 1909.

Wallace, Lew. *An Autobiography,* Vol. 2. New York: Harper, 1906.

Wallace, Susan E. *The Land of the Pueblos.* Troy: Nims & Knight, 1889.

Wallace, William S. *A Journey Through New Mexico's First Judicial District, in 1864; Letters to the Editor of the Santa Fe Weekly New Mexico.* Los Angeles: Westernlore Press, 1956.

The War of the Rebellion. A compilation of the Official Records of the Union and Confederate Armies. Series I, II, III. Washington: Government Printing Office, 1880.

Webb, Walter Prescott. *The Great Plains.* Boston: Ginn & Co., 1931.

Whitford, William Clarke. *Colorado Volunteers in the Civil War; the New Mexico Campaign in 1862.* Denver: State Historical and Natural History Society, 1906.

Woodward, Dorothy. *New Mexico, Land of Enchantment.* 77th Congress, 1st session. Senate Document 91. Washington: Government Printing Office, 1941.

Index

THE author wishes to thank President John F. Kennedy for preparing the Foreword to "New Mexico's Troubled Years." He also expresses his appreciation to the following persons for their important contributions to the progress of the book: Clinton P. Anderson, Caroline Davis, Roland F. Dickey, George Fitzpatrick, William A. Keleher, and William S. Wallace.

The Palace of the Governors in Santa Fe.
From a pencil sketch by Lew Wallace in
The Land of the Pueblos, by Susan E. Wallace, 1889.